MAKING CONCRETE GARDEN ORNAMENTS

MAKING CONCRETE GARDEN ORNAMENTS

Sherri Warner Hunter

LARK BOOKS

A Division of Sterling Publishing Co., Inc.
New York

Acknowledgments

Writing this book has given me a new-found appreciation of how many people and how much energy it takes to produce a book; I'm grateful to so many that have provided support, guidance, and information along the way; however, there are a few specific names I want to acknowledge.

I'd like to thank my contributing designers Elder Jones, Lynn Olson, and George Adamy for their technical advice and assistance, as well as for their passion for creating. Thank you also to Andrew Goss, for his generosity in allowing me to use his Concrete and Metal website as a source of inspiration and information.

A very special thank you to my editor, Joe Rhatigan, whose patience, prodding, good work, and sense of humor helped me to do the work that needed to be done. Cool beans! Thank you to art director Celia Naranjo, who not only designs beautiful books, but knows how to leave her mark on concrete as well. I have great appreciation for the eye and comments of photographer Evan Bracken, and for the attention to detail by Assistant Editor Veronika Gunter.

There were several locations used to photograph the projects, and I'd like to thank those fine folks for letting up invade their beautiful yards and gardens: Ray and Susan Allen, Murfreesboro, TN; Randy and Lisa McCurdy, Wartrace, TN; Kim Brooks and Rusty Wolfe at Finer Things Gallery, Nashville, TN; and Jimmy and Dale White, Weaverville, NC. I also want to thank The North Carolina Arboretum, Asheville, NC for providing wonderful locations for the photographs on pages 2, 100, 115, 117, and 140.

Valuable assistance and support was provided by Tiffany Cataldo Delk and Kristina Bell in the development of projects and continued studio efforts with the help of Janet Cataldo and Pam Brown as I sat facing the computer screen. For inspiration along the way, thank you to my dad, Dr. Robert S. Warner, Mary Mark Munday, Willem Volkersz, and the late Dale Eldred, all, in their own way over the years have helped to guide me down my concrete path. And for his assistance, patience, love, and friendship, I'm forever thankful to my partner and husband, Martin.

Editor: **Joe Rhatigan**
Art director: **Celia Naranjo**
Cover design: **Rob Pulleyn**
Photography: **Evan Bracken**
Illustrations: **Orrin Lundgren**
Production assistant: **Hannes Charen**
Assistant editor: **Veronika Alice Gunter**

Library of Congress Cataloging-in-Publication Data
Hunter, Sherri Warner.
    Creating with concrete : yard art, sculpture, and garden
    projects / Sherri Warner Hunter.
        p. cm.
    ISBN 1-57990-179-4 (hardcover)   ISBN 1-57990-318-5 (paperback)
    1. Garden ornaments and furniture—Design and construction.
        2. Concrete. I. Title.

SB473.5 .H865 2001
717—dc21   00-053471

10 9 8 7 6 5 4 3 2 1

Published by Lark Books, a division of Sterling Publishing Co., Inc.
387 Park Avenue South, New York, N.Y. 10016

© 2001, Sherri Warner Hunter

Distributed in Canada by Sterling Publishing,
c/o Canadian Manda Group, One Atlantic Ave., Suite 105
Toronto, Ontario, Canada M6K 3E7

Distributed in the U.K. by:
Guild of Master Craftsman Publications Ltd.
Castle Place, 166 High Street, Lewes East Sussex, England BN7 1XU
Tel: (+ 44) 1273 477374, Fax: (+ 44) 1273 478606,
Email: pubs@thegmcgroup.com, Web: www.gmcpublications.com

Distributed in Australia by Capricorn Link (Australia) Pty Ltd.,
P.O. Box 704, Windsor, NSW 2756 Australia

If you have questions or comments about this book, please contact:
Lark Books
67 Broadway
Asheville, NC 28801
(828) 236-9730

Printed in China

ISBN 1-57990-179-4 (hardcover)   ISBN 1-57990-318-5 (paperback)

Table of Contents

Concrete Isn't Just for Sidewalks Anymore

Just look around you: colorful polished concrete in
public plazas, concrete
sculptural forms rising from hills,
gold-leafed concrete jewelry,
ferro-cement boats in the ocean,
photographic images on exposed
aggregate concrete walls. Concrete, once used primarily as a
great building material, is now
looked at as an elegant, versatile
material anyone can manipulate
to express themselves artistically.
Concrete is just beginning to
receive the attention it deserves,
and I am proud to be able to
show you some of the amazing
things you can do with it to create functional and decorative
pieces for your yard or garden.
Whether you're an experienced
sculptor or someone looking for a
way to express your creativity,
concrete will provide you with a
lifetime of creative possibilities.
Forget what you *think* you know
about concrete; you're in for a
surprise.

Marvin and Lilli Ann Killen Rosenberg, *Walkway with Planter*, 2000, Stephen's Place Affordable
Housing Project, Medford, OR. Colored concrete fish; slate, mosaics, inlaid shells, stones, and bones.
Photo by Marvin Rosenberg

Andrew Goss, *Three Pins*, 1999, 2 x 3 x ½ inches (5.1 x 7.6 x 1.3 cm). Fine mix of stone dust, cement, latex, and fibers, cast in modeling clay; 24-karat gold leaf. Photo by Kris Rosar

Looking Back

Ever since man started building stone structures, he's experimented with mixtures to create a binding agent. Early civilizations used clay. The Egyptians made a mortar using lime and gypsum to construct the pyramids. The Greeks continued to make improvements; however, it was the Romans who finally developed a cement that combined *slaked lime*, lime which had been broken down and combined with water, and volcanic ash. Simultaneously, similar construction advances were occurring in early civilizations in Mexico and Central America. After the fall of the Roman Empire, this technique was lost until 1756, when a British engineer, John Smeaton, invented a hydraulic cement made from limestone containing a considerable proportion of clay. In 1824, Joseph Aspdin, another Englishman who was a bricklayer and mason, patented the manufacturing of a hydraulic cement that involved mixing a careful proportion of limestone and clay, pulverizing and burning (firing in a kiln) the mixture, which was then ground to a fine powder. He called his product *portland cement* because, when hardened, its color resembled the high-quality limestone that was quarried on the Isle of Portland off the British coast.

The first portland cement manufactured in the United States is credited to David O. Saylor, in Coplay, Pennsylvania, in 1871. The firing of the materials took place in a crude burning chamber. Again an Englishman advanced the industry's technology when F. Ransome engineered and patented a specialized kiln to process the materials. In 1902, Thomas Edison further developed the kiln, leading to significant increases in concrete production and its popularity as a construction material. Edison realized the versatility of portland cement and even used it to make cast furniture. A consummate craftsman, his first piece was an early phonograph cabinet detailed with elaborate scroll work.

Roy Kanwit, *Two Pregnant Women*, 1998, 7 x 5 x 2 feet (2.1 x 1.5 x .6 m). Ferro cement modeled over steel frame; surface treatment includes dyes, polishing, acrylic sealant. Photo by artist

Jack Hastings, *Sculpture Garden*, Chattanooga Welcome Center, Interstate 75, Chattanooga, TN. Wet-carved concrete. Photo by artist

Looking Forward

As the modern age advances, trained professionals in the building industry and in art and architecture continue to explore the possible applications of concrete. The gallery artists included in this book represent some of the many ways that concrete is being used. Techniques are invented and then improved over time. Elder Jones (see his projects on pages 84, 102, 121, and 134) has spent his career refining the wet carving of concrete, a technique he learned from his mentor, Jack Hastings, who was inspired by the work of Constantino Nivola (1911-1988), a pioneer in this technique. Typical

Elder G. Jones, *Southwestern Pot*, 2000, 10 x 13½ x 11½ inches (25.4 x 34.3 x 29.2 cm). Carved concrete with iron oxide tint. Photo by artist

construction uses of concrete have inspired artists such as Lorado Taft (1860-1936), who, having studied how modern buildings were cast in concrete, used concrete to create large-scale figurative sculptures that would be prohibitively expensive to create in any other medium. In fact, modern architecture is a major source of inspiration for many artists working in concrete. I can't help but look in awe at a construction site—I think of it as a great big sculpture. When I see good designs combined with caring craftsmanship at all levels, from the way the try wire holds the rebar together, to the construction of the curved forms for the walls, I'm inspired as I return to my own work. Today, I work with concrete extensively, and nothing gives me as much joy. Whether it's a large-scale public sculpture or a small fountain, I feel that concrete has given me the versatility I've always sought in a material. And I look forward to sharing the results of my years of experimentation and discovery with you.

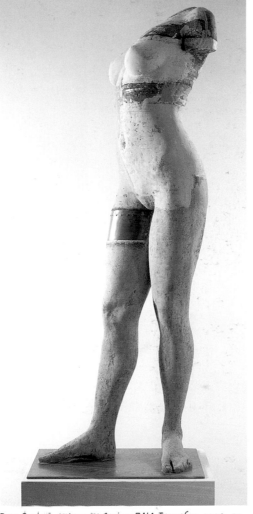

Dan Corbin, *Integrity Series: DNA Transfer*, 2000, 54 x 15 x 10 inches (137.2 x 38.1 x 25.4 cm). Cement, oxides, paint, sheet metals; casting, cut, and stacked; embedding, sanding, painting. Photo by artist

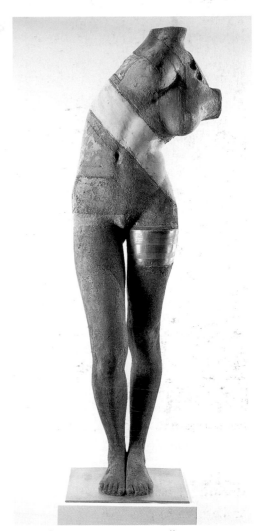

Dan Corbin, *Opposition Series: Yellow Brown*, 1999, 53 x 18 x 10 inches (134.6 x 45.7 x 25.4 cm). Cement, oxides, paint, sheet metals, casting, cut, and stacked; embedding, sanding, painting. Photo by artist

George E. Adamy, *Black & Gold Balls*, 1990, diameters of 4½ and 6½ inches (11.4 and 16.5 cm). Portland cement, sand, glass scrim, Polyadam II; castings in molds made from rubber balls; colored with iridescent acrylics. Photo by artist

Andrew Goss, *Cloud/Fish*, 2000, 10 x 32 x 6 inches (25.4 x 81.3 x 15.2 cm). Concrete, copper rod, stainless steel wire, brass; built up over mesh, filled with white portland cement and sanded. Photo by artist

Lynn Olson, *Sitting Puppy*, 1998, 24 x 18 x 12 inches (61 x 45.7 x 30.5 cm). Cement, stainless steel, carbon fibers; direct modeling; pigments for color, polished, sealed with methyl methacrylate. Photo by artist

Buddy Rhodes, *Sphere Planter*, 2000, 4 feet tall (1.2 m). Cement, sand, and binders; pressed concrete into molds; colored concrete backfilled with contrasting concrete; ground, sanded, and sealed. Photo by Buddy Rhodes Studio

Elder G. Jones, *Coiled Pot*, 1999, 19 x 15½ inches (48.3 x 39.4 cm). Carved concrete. Photo by artist

Left: Johan Hagaman, *Bound by Words*, 1999, 30 x 14 x 9 inches (76.2 x 35.6 x 22.9 cm). Concrete, steel wire, bronze wire, polyester resin, rope light; direct modeling over an armature of foam core and wire; embedded words written into concrete formed with bronze wire, and glass; cured cement stained with acid-based stain. Photo by artist

Bottom left: Sherri Warner Hunter, *Fashion Lady* (fountain),1997; 3 feet (90 cm) tall; concrete over an armature shaped with wire mesh; sand-cast bowl; surface treatments include embedding and direct modeling. Photo by artist

Below: Nina Solomon and Sue Chenoweth, *From the Round Earth's Imagined Corners*, 2000, installation in Phoenix, AZ. 37 1/2 x 19 1/2 x 21 inches (95.3 x 49.5 x 53.3 cm). Welded steel armature, polystyrene foam, fiberglass mesh, cement and polymer admix; foam glued to armature with construction cement, covered with medium mesh, cement, then large mesh sewed in place with telephone wire on seat, seatback, and legs, covered with final coat cement; handmade stoneware tiles of animals used for mosaic covering, tiles applied with thin-set mortar, charcoal grout. Photo by James Cowlin

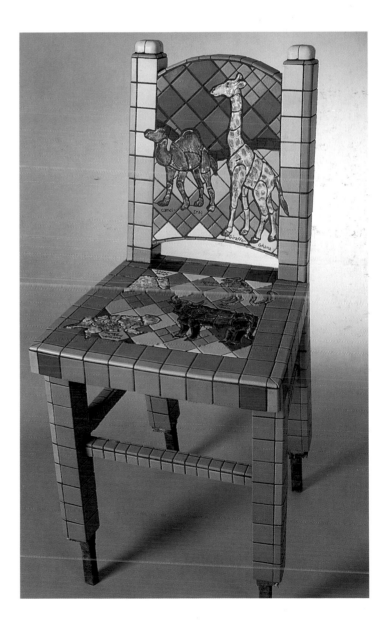

Marvin and Lilli Ann Killen Rosenberg, *Frog Water Fountain*, 1996, St. Christopher's Children's Hospital, Philadelphia, PA. Concrete with mosaic and ceramic pieces over rebar and wire mesh. Photo by Ken Wittenberg

Pedro Silva, *The Mother and Baby Sea Serpent*, 1981, Fanny Mae Dee Park, Nashville, TN (also known as Dragon Park). Concrete hand formed over a steel and mesh armature and then covered in mosaic designs created by hundreds of community volunteers. Photo by Sherri Warner Hunter

Tom Arie Donch, *Turtle Emerging from Wall*, 1997, Brevard Zoo, FL. 66 x 60 x 78 inches (1.7 x 1.5 x 2 m). Concrete hand formed over a steel and mesh armature; color applied by mixing pigments into the concrete. Photo by artist

Tom Arie Donch, *Shark*, 1993, 54 x 42 x 162 inches (1.4 x 1 x 4 m). Concrete hand formed over a steel and mesh armature; color applied by mixing pigments into the concrete. Photo by artist

Sherri Warner Hunter, *Flights of Fancy*, 1996, Nashville International Airport, Nashville, TN. 3 x 23 x 26 feet (.9 x 7 x 8 m). Ceramic and glass mosaic over reinforced concrete forms. Photo by Gary Layda

Right: Jack Hastings, *Ready Kilowatt*, 1992, 60 × 36 inches (1.5 × .9 m). Sprayed cement over an armature. Photo by artist

Below left: Johan Hagaman, *Bird Fountain*, 1999, 39 × 13 × 17 inches (99.1 × 33 × 43.2 cm). Concrete, iron hinges, water pump. Photo by artist

Below right: Roy Kanwit, *Gaia (Mother Earth)*, 1994, 19¼ × 10 × 22 feet (5.7 × 3 × 6.6 m). Ferro-cement direct modeled over steel frame. Photo by artist

Concrete Basics

Simply put, concrete is a mixture of cement, water, and aggregate, which is the bulk material needed to make concrete.

The Ingredients of Concrete

The cement and water mix together and start a chemical process known as *hydration*, which causes the concrete to harden. Concrete does not dry; it cures through the hydration process. Freshly applied concrete should be kept damp and cool to ensure that this process proceeds slowly and completely. If water is allowed to evaporate too quickly from the concrete, the finished piece will be weak and might crack.

The fun begins as you master the basic principles of mixing and forming and learn how to manipulate the concrete to achieve creative and unique constructions.

CEMENT

For the projects in this book, you'll be using the most common type of cement, portland cement, type I. There are five types of portland cement, each represented by the Roman numerals I through V. Type I is typically used for general construction purposes.

Portland cement is easy to find and readily available at hardware stores,

Gray and white portland cement

home improvement centers, and building supply yards. Most often, it comes packaged in a water-resistant paper bag weighing 94 pounds (43 kg). Check the bag when you buy cement; never buy one that's open or has a hole in it. Cement starts absorbing moisture as soon as the bag is opened. If a bag feels hard as a rock, try another.

Although cement may become compressed in the bag during shipping and storage, a little agitation should return it to its powdery consistency. Lumpy or hard cement is useless, so try to buy your cement from a source that receives new stock regularly, so you're buying fresh materials. Cement is cheap, but the work you put into your project is what gives it value. Always work with the best quality materials you can to ensure the finest results.

Typically, portland cement is gray, though you might notice slight shade variations from different manufacturers. There is also a white portland cement that is produced through additional refining. It's as structurally sound as the gray and might be desirable in some applications, especially when working with coloring agents. You'll achieve a purer color mixing pigments into white rather than gray cement. White portland costs about twice as much as the gray and may not be available at all sources.

AGGREGATES

Aggregates are the bulk material added to the cement to make concrete. An aggregate can be any number of materials including sand,

Materials clockwise from top center: aquarium gravel, crushed gravel, gravel, vermiculite, masonry sand, pea gravel, pool mix. Center: potting soil made of perlite and peat moss

gravel, crushed stone, and even lightweight materials, such as *vermiculite* and *perlite*. Vermiculite and perlite are naturally mined materials that are processed by heat to expand. They're commonly used by builders as insulation, and by gardeners as additives to potting soils to help with aeration and drainage.

The cost, quality, and working properties of your concrete will be affected by the kind of aggregate you use. If you plan to model with concrete, you wouldn't include large rocks in your mix—you'd use masonry sand for a smoother texture. If you're pouring a slab or base that will bear weight or support a structure, a well-graded mix of gravel will provide added strength. A well-graded mix of aggregate includes various sizes of crushed rock or gravel and sand. The smaller sizes of gravel shift to fill in spaces between larger ones, while the sand particles fill in the smallest areas. The cement paste coats each piece of aggregate and hardens the mixture into a solid mass (figure 1). Hydration begins when water is added to cement, and molecules form on the surfaces of the aggregates to provide the strength of

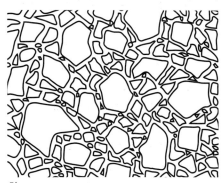

Figure 1

the material. Sharp aggregates aid in creating a strong bond because it's easier for the molecule to form on the flat surfaces. Crushed rock is sharper than river rock, and masonry sand is sharper than play sand (see chart on page 17).

Aggregates usually cost less than concrete, so the "bulk" factor may mean money savings. Along those lines, concrete that has a high ratio of cement to aggregate is often referred to as "rich," since the cement costs more by volume than the aggregate.

Regardless of the type of aggregate you choose, the materials should be clean and free of dirt, clay, plants, or other organic materials. These foreign particles prevent the cement paste from binding to the aggregate, and may produce an inferior grade of concrete.

In the building industry, aggregates are rated by size using a number system. The lower the number, the coarser the material. The size, color, and sharpness of your aggregate is going to change the appearance, workability, and cost of your mix. Different manufacturers and regional suppliers may provide variations of common materials. Maybe pink marble chips are available in your area, but crushed shells are impossible to find. Even unlikely leftovers from manufacturing, such as metal shavings, carborundum dust, or sawdust can be utilized as aggregates to create a specialty mix.

WATER

Use clean water to mix your concrete. A good rule of thumb is, if you can drink it, it's good enough to mix with. Don't use muddy, oily, or toxic liquids to mix your concrete. If you plan to use sea water to mix with concrete, you may want to reconsider. The finished structure will start out strong; however, it'll weaken over time due to the salt content. The salt also causes an increase of surface moisture and *efflorescence* (the white residue that naturally occurs in concrete due to lime and salts), and shouldn't be used where surface appearance is important or where concrete is to be painted or plastered. Beach sand should be avoided as an aggregate because the salt in the sand will cause the same problems.

ADMIXTURES

An *admixture* is any additional material added to the mix other than cement, aggregates, and water.

Materials clockwise from upper left: alkali resistant fiberglass mesh (glass scrim) beneath container of acrylic polymer fortifier (milk), polypropolene fibers and polyester fibers atop light/medium alkali-resistant fiberglass mesh (glass scrim), container of air-entrainment agent

	TYPE OF AGGREGATE	WHERE TO FIND	QUALITIES
COARSE TO MEDIUM: Stone	Crushed gravel/rock	Building supply, home improvement center	Gray, angular
	Marble chips	Building supply, garden center, marble manufacturer	Most often white to gray, luminous
	Pea gravel	Building supply, home improvement center	Natural, rounded
	River rock	Building supply, home improvement center, river beds	Natural brown tones, rounded
FINE: Silica/Sand	Masonry sand	Building supply	Sharp, light in color— usually ordered in bulk
	Play sand	Home improvement center	Available in bags
	Marble sand	Building supply	Fine white sand, also called swimming pool mix
EXTREMELY FINE	Silica fume	Manufacturer	A waste product from metal smelting—very fine dark powder; Increases density but tricky to work with
	Metakaolin	Manufacturer	White powder
MISCELLANEOUS	Vermiculite	Garden center	Expanded mica
	Perlite	Garden center	Pulverized, expanded plastic
	Aquarium gravel	Pet center	Natural or colored, dyed gravel
	Crushed shells	Manufacturer, nature	Textural, colorful

Admixes are used in concrete for a variety of reasons, including modifying its set time, improving its workability, or adding color. Some of the most common admixtures used in concrete today are *air-entraining agents*, which are soap-like substances that produce a large number of microscopic bubbles or voids in the cement paste, making the freshly mixed concrete more workable. These small voids also provide needed space for the moisture in concrete to expand and contract during freeze/thaw cycles, which makes air-entraining agents highly beneficial for major construction projects like roads, runways, and bridges. This special additive must be combined in a careful ratio with the water and then mixed mechanically with the cement and aggregate to work effectively. Mixing it in by hand doesn't provide enough agitation to be effective.

Latex polymer additives also provide moisture resistance, workability, and durability. Specifics on various admixtures will be explored in the Custom Recipes section on pages 28 and 29.

PREMIXED CONCRETE
There are companies that specialize in prepackaged dry concrete mixes. Different types of dry concrete mixes are available in 40, 60, or 80-pound (18.2, 27.2, or 36.3 kg) bags. Basically, all you do is add water and stir. These mixes are great for certain projects, and there is the advantage of not having to store separate ingredients. The two main disadvantages are that you're paying a premium for your materials, and you're not able to customize the mix. The materials list for each project will indicate when a premix can be substituted for a customized mix.

When you visit the concrete aisle of your home improvement center, you'll probably be surprised by the wide variety of packaged material available. A word of caution: I use the word "concrete" generically throughout this book. You don't want to buy the premixed concrete for the projects. Look specifically for the Sand or Topping Mix or the Mortar Mix as specified.

READY MIX

Ready mix is concrete that is prepared at a plant and loaded onto a truck for delivery. Once the truck gets to the job site, it begins to pour or pump large quantities of concrete. For the projects contained in this book, I won't be recommending quantities that will make this necessary.

Concrete tools top row: rubber float, rub block. Center row: putty knife, serrated plastic putty knife, garden trowel, pointing trowel, small hoe. Bottom row: coarse file, wire brush, rifflers, paint brush, wood chisel, steel trowel, 4½- inch (11.4 cm) grinder with masonry cutting blade

Tools and Equipment

Working concrete has a long, honorable tradition, and the basic tools used by trade professionals will come in handy. You may already have many tools in your garage or work space you can use for working with concrete. Over time, you'll find yourself fabricating or adapting many things to use as tools as you develop your own finishing techniques. Specialized tools used in several of the techniques will be listed separately in Chapters 2 and 3.

CONCRETE TOOLS

Don't be intimidated by this list. You can get started with a pair of rubber gloves and a plastic dish tub. As you continue your exploration of con-

crete, you may want to invest in tools specifically suited for your projects.

Mixers and Mixing Containers: The type of mixer you use will depend on the quantity of concrete you'll need for the project. Concrete can easily be mixed by hand on a simple sheet

Plastic dish tubs and containers

of plywood, a high-sided wheelbarrow, or a mortar box. When working with larger quantities or certain types of additives, a gas or electric mixer might be the way to go. For most projects, I like to use a wheelbarrow so I can easily transport the

Mortar box, mortar hoe, and shovels

concrete to my work area, but if I'm just mixing up a small quantity, I'll use a plastic dish tub. A plastic mixing container with rounded edges makes it easier to mix ingredients thoroughly, and it'll be easier to clean afterwards.

Another mixer recently appeared on the market. Basically it's the size of a 5-gallon (19 L) bucket with two flanges on the interior and a lid that screws on with a seal. You add your ingredients, screw on the lid, and roll it on the ground. It's great exercise, and if there's a young child around who wants to help, it's a good way to have them work off some energy. I've had great results with this mixer.

Shovels: Experienced professionals use shovels to measure materials, but more often, you'll use a shovel to place concrete or dig a form.

Mortar Hoe: Even a garden hoe will work to mix concrete. The advantage of this specialized hoe, however, is that it has two large holes in the blade that allow the ingredients to flow through the blade as you push and pull the hoe through the mixture.

Screed: This isn't a fancy tool you buy. It's the official name of a straight board that is used for the initial *striking off* or leveling of poured or cast forms. The process is called *screeding*.

Wooden Float: A float is a short, rectangular tool used in the first stage of finishing the surface on concrete. It can also be used as the only finishing tool if a rougher surface is desired.

Steel Trowel: While this tool is called a trowel, it's actually rectangular and is used in finishing concrete for a smooth, polished surface. I sometimes use this tool for other than its intended purpose, and instead, use it as a hawk to hold a quantity of concrete.

Mason's or Brick Trowel and Pointing Trowel: These are the tools we most often associate with bricklayers. They're typically diamond shaped, but can also be rectangular. They're useful in placing or delivering concrete to a specific area.

Rub Brick: This is an abrasive brick with a handle used to knock off concrete burrs and bumps, or to smooth edges.

WOODWORKING TOOLS

For many of the projects, you'll be building either a form or mold to pour the concrete into, or an armature or frame to apply the concrete onto. Obviously, for every power tool, there is a hand version of that tool. I love tools, so every chance I get, I add a new one to my collection.

Power Saws: Any type of saw, rang-

ing from a circular saw to a table saw, radial arm saw, band saw or even a jigsaw, can be a big time saver and useful for cutting boards for forms or molds. A band saw is also great for cutting polystyrene foam.

Power Drill: If you're just starting to compile tools for your shop or studio, a good power drill is the most versatile and useful tool to have on hand. Different accessories including screwdriver heads, wire wheels, and mixer attachments make this tool much more useful than for just drilling holes.

Fasteners: It's always helpful to have an assortment of wood and metal fasteners on hand. A few of the types we'll be using regularly for the projects include drywall screws, galvanized roofing nails, and common nails.

Other tools to have on hand include a short-handled sledgehammer or mallet, a construction-grade claw hammer, a tape measure, and a steel try square.

METALWORKING TOOLS

Besides investing in a good metal hacksaw or power cutoff saw and a 4½-inch (11.4 cm) grinder with metal grinding wheels, which can also be used as a metal-cutting tool, it would be good to have the following tools handy as well:

Lineman's Pliers: These are particularly strong jawed pliers that will help you get a good grip for tightening wires. Each pair has a built-in wire cutter as well.

Angle Cutters: Angle cutters have one job and they do it well—to cut wire clean and close.

Aviator Shears: Aviator shears look like a cross between a heavy pair of scissors and a pair of pliers. Unlike tin snips, aviator shears have a built-in spring action to help with cutting sheet metal and metal meshes, such as hardware cloth and chicken wire.

Setting Up Your Work Area

Maybe you've driven past a construction site and seen a pile of sand with a shovel sticking out of it, a pallet of cement wrapped in plastic, a hose, and a well-used mixer all grouped together—everything conveniently close at hand. You want to do the same thing as you set up your work area.

Power cutoff saw

The work area will be different for virtually everyone who reads this book. It may be a shady spot under a tree or in your driveway, a corner of your garage or patio, or a workshop or studio. Regardless of where your work area is or how big it is, the main considerations are simple:

1. Do you have easy access to materials for mixing, and water for cleanup?

2. Is the work area (or the project) protected from extreme weather conditions during construction and curing?

3. Can you work on your project in a position that will not cause physical strain?

Let me share with you how I've addressed those concerns, and maybe that'll help you define your work area.

I frequently work with concrete, so I keep an inventory of about eight bags of cement on hand. In order to keep it fresh, they're stacked on a wooden pallet close to my studio door (remember, these bags weigh 94 pounds [43 kg] each). The pallet keeps them off the damp floor. Additionally, I first lay down a large sheet of plastic, stack the bags, and cover them with the plastic when not in use. If your work space is limited, you might consider storing one bag at a time, in its original packaging, in a plastic trash bag or trash can. How you receive and store your sand also depends on your situation. I like to have my sand delivered in bulk, so periodically a large dump truck backs up to my studio and delivers a couple of tons of sharp, white masonry sand. I keep the sand pile covered with a tarp to discourage my cat and keep out debris. I still have to be careful not to scoop up the occasional frog or lizard who thinks they've found the ideal vacation

Tools clockwise from top left: leather work gloves, 4½-inch (11.4 cm) grinder with metal grinding wheel, slip-jaw pliers, lineman's pliers, bolt cutters, hacksaw, small hacksaw, metal file, angle wire cutters, needle-nose pliers, aviator shears

Everything you need should be conveniently located.

spot. Of course, storing this much sand isn't practical for everyone. Fortunately, sand is usually available wherever you purchase your cement. More often, you'll find "play" sand. It'll work, but try to find a source for masonry sand if you can.

I have a hose connection on the outside of my studio as my water source. Since I don't have running water inside the studio, I just keep a supply of large containers filled to use as needed.

Most of the tools and supplies I use for working with concrete are organized in one area of my studio, so that my set-up time is minimized and I can concentrate on the work.

I work on a sturdy table and cover as much of the work area as possible with sheets of plastic. This makes for an easy cleanup at the end of each work session. If I'm working on a large piece on the floor, I cover the area under and around the piece with plastic to maintain the quality of my studio floor. In situations where I'm working on a piece on site or in its final location, I take care to keep the area as clean as possible during the construction process, removing any debris after each work session. That provides both a safe and efficient work space.

Whenever possible, I position a project on a work board. The type of work board you'll want to use depends on the project. For some casting projects, I select a wooden board of ³/₄-inch (1.9 cm) plywood, and cover it with 4 mil plastic. In these instances, the sheet plastic also functions as a smooth surface to cast on. If you're carving a cast form, working on a piece of hard plastic sheeting provides a nonstick surface that's easy to clean and can hold up to the rigors of the process.

WORKING IN THE ROUND

When working on three-dimensional pieces, it's very important to be able to work all the way around the piece, often referred to as "working in the round." The primary goal of the sculptor is to create pieces of work that are interesting and successful from all viewing angles. Many of the projects presented in this book are sculptural in nature, and you want to make them interesting from all vantage points. There are several methods you can use to help you physically work your pieces in the round.

Larger pieces can be placed directly on the floor or ground so you can walk and work around them. A medium-sized piece can be positioned on a work board at the corner of your worktable so that you're always able to work on two-thirds of the piece at a time. It's always better to rotate the work board rather than the actual piece. Rotating a work board is made easier by positioning a smaller board under the work board. Better yet, you can rotate your piece and its work board on a heavy-duty metal turntable or a sturdy lazy Susan.

Sometimes we get so involved with a piece or a project that we forget to step back and view the piece in its entirety. Periodically, remember to stop and look, really look, at what you're doing.

Cleaning Up

Cleaning up after working with concrete isn't like cleaning up after a meatloaf dinner—leaving things to soak won't help. I keep 5-gallon (19 L) buckets filled with water at all times for rinsing my gloves, hands, and tools. I'd do this even if I had a sink nearby, because you don't want to rinse concrete down your drain. As a hydraulic material, it'll continue to set underwater or in your drainpipes, wreaking havoc on your plumbing. By handling your cleanup in the buckets, you can let the concrete residue settle overnight, pour off the water, and discard the sludge into the trash. Use a hose to clean out your wheelbarrow or mixer. Just don't let the concrete go down your pipes!

Wash and dry metal tools, and treat them with a light spray lubricant to inhibit rusting.

Safety

Safe work habits also mean good health habits. One of the key components of concrete is silica. When inhaled over long periods of time, silica particles will affect your sinuses and lungs. Buy the best particle dust mask you can, and wear it *every time* you're mixing dry components, sanding, drilling, or doing anything else that creates dust from the concrete or its components. If you intend to save the mask in between uses, store it in a sealed plastic bag. A dust mask left sitting on an open shelf may collect more dust than it protects you from. Plus, don't share your dust mask with anyone else.

Always wear a good pair of rubber or latex gloves when working with concrete to protect your hands from the caustic chemicals in the cement and abrasions from the aggregate. The

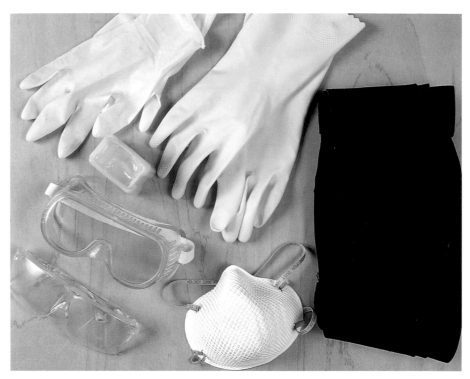

Safety materials clockwise from top left: latex surgical-style gloves, heavy-duty latex gloves, back brace, dust mask, goggles

quality and cost of gloves can vary. I've found that the flocked-lined, yellow latex gloves that are available in supermarket cleaning aisles work well. I also keep a quantity of the lightweight, surgical-style latex gloves on hand to wear when I'm working on details or surface treatments, such as modeling or embedding.

Another quality of concrete is that it draws moisture from wherever it can, including your skin. After a day's work, when you wash your hands, they may feel a little slippery, even slimy. Don't be fooled. Without a good dose of hand cream, you'll feel the drying effects. Find a good hand cream and use it.

Wear work clothes you can get good and dirty. Also, take a hint from your local home improvement center employee, and wear a good back support, particularly if you know your back is weak. Throughout the process of mixing, creating, and moving your work, practice safe lifting procedures: lift with your legs, not your back.

Goggles are necessary to wear for many different stages, from working with power tools to building your forms and molds, to some of the techniques that involve carving or grinding concrete. Always use safe work practices, but mostly, use good common sense.

Mixing Concrete

You have two choices when it comes to mixing concrete: mix it by hand or mix it by machine. When you're working on small projects, mixing by hand is the easiest approach. You can keep your quantities small, and cleanup is relatively easy. If you're planning to use an air-entraining agent, you have to use a machine, because hand mixing isn't going to provide the agitation needed to create the air bubbles.

Whatever mixing method you choose, always take care as you add the water to your mix. Only use as much water as needed to make the mix a workable consistency for the techniques you're using.

DETERMINING QUANTITIES

All recipes for concrete will specify *parts* for the various ingredients you'll use in a mix. The parts are indications of volume. It doesn't matter what you use to measure the volume of your ingredients, but it's important to use the same measure for all of your ingredients. A trade professional might use a shovel to measure, another person might use a box or a bucket. For small quantities, I use recycled plastic food containers, such as butter tubs or cottage cheese containers. Whatever you use, continue to use that for the entire batch you're mixing. Also, don't pack the materials into your measure—scoop loosely.

Ideally, you want to mix just the right amount of concrete for your project so that you have enough, without too much leftover. Simple enough goal. I asked a number of artists how they calculate the quantities they mix, and I received as many different answers. There's the mathematical approach. Concrete is calculated in cubic amounts: cubic feet, cubic yards, cubic centimeters, and so on. For smaller molds and forms, you can multiply the surface area by the height of the mold for cubic inches and then divide by 1,728 to arrive at a cubic foot calculation to use as you measure your quantities (multiply the result by .03 to convert to cubic meters).

Another method, one that isn't quite so math dependent, is to fill your mold or form with the aggregate you'll be using. If you're using sand for a mix to cast a stepping-stone, fill your stepping-stone mold with sand. Measure the sand and then calculate your cement proportions based on that measurement. The volume of concrete adds very little bulk since the small concrete particles mixed in water go in between the aggregate particles.

It's a good idea to keep a record in either a journal or sketchbook as you develop your working methods. Once you have worked out just the right amount of concrete needed to fill a favorite mold, write down what you used to measure your ingredients and how many parts. As you continue to explore forms in concrete, you might want to write down other useful information, such as how long it took for a certain mixture to set, or how long a mixture remained workable for a specific technique. Your personal experience will make the information provided here even more useful.

Determine the quantity of concrete you'll be working with, and decide on the appropriate mixing container. Mix a quantity you can easily use and finish within two hours or less. Both the temperature and humidity will affect the amount of work time you have. If you're pouring a form, err on the side of mixing too much concrete. You don't want to be close to filling a form only to find that you need to stop to mix up an extra batch of concrete to top it off. It's not unusual, however, to mix multiple batches of concrete for larger projects. If you have concrete leftover, you might try to have some additional molds handy to utilize the excess concrete. One artist I know is slowly adding onto a patio with his leftover material.

MIXING CONCRETE BY HAND

Mixing by hand will work for most projects. Remember to wear your gloves and dust mask as you're measuring and mixing the dry ingredients. Measure the dry ingredients into your mixing container, starting first with the aggregate, then the cement. The powdery cement sticks to the sides of the mixing container if put in first. Then, thoroughly mix the dry materials with your hands or a tool, until the mixture is uniform in color and consistency. Make a depression in the center of the dry materials, and pour in three quarters of the suggested proportion of water, and mix. Make sure that you incorporate all the dried material at the bottom and edges of your container. Slowly add the final one-quarter measure of water as you mix, until you achieve the desired consistency.

Measuring the amount of water is tricky. For one thing, you can never measure the exact amount that you'll use—the amount of water needed will vary with the amount of moisture in the sand, the humidity, and even the temperature of your tools and materials. I'll provide you with a recommended amount of water for each concrete mix recipe, but use caution as you add the final amount of water.

Ideally, you'll use the least amount of water needed to make the mixture the desired consistency for the process you're trying to achieve. Some mixes require more water than others. Too much water in the mix may make a finished piece weak; if the mix is too dry, it may not finish out well or flow into the edges of a casting properly.

MIXING BY MACHINE

When you're mixing with a power mixer, start with half of the recommended water, add all of your aggregate, and then add the cement as the mixer is rotating. Slowly add the balance of the water, observing the consistency carefully. Your mix may not require the full measure of water. Stop when the desired consistency is reached, and note the adjusted proportions, particularly if you'll be working on one project with multiple batches. You want them to be the same consistency.

For ready-to-use mixes, follow the instructions on the bag.

WORKING STAGES

As you work with concrete, the consistency of the concrete mix will be the key to success. The same recipe may be mixed at different consistencies to achieve different results. A sand mix may be mixed with slightly more water to achieve a batter-like consistency so that it flows more easily into the corners of a mold, while the same ingredients with less water can be mixed to a clay-like consistency to effectively apply onto an armature.

Top left: Measure your dry ingredients starting with the sand (aggregate). Top right: Mix the ingredients together thoroughly. Bottom left and right: Add just enough water until the mix is the proper consistency for the technique you're using.

Electric concrete mixer

After the concrete ingredients are mixed, there are different set points or stages when the hydration process has started and the concrete has begun to transform. These set stages will have another effect on the workable consistency. At the different set stages, different types of manipulation or finishing can occur. After about the first 20 to 30 minutes, the initial set has occurred, and you'll notice the concrete getting firmer. As it continues to firm, you may find it difficult to proceed with the technique you're working on. The general rule is never to re-temper or add water to your mix. I must admit there are times when I'm close to finishing a layer of concrete or have just a little more detail I want to complete without mixing a new batch. I add the smallest amount of water—a spray from a water bottle to mist the surface—and then manage to mix without serious consequences. But this is not a recommended practice.

Within two to four hours, a cast piece will be firm. The water that has collected on the surface (bleeding) will have evaporated, and while the piece will feel firm, it will not be hard. This firm set stage is usually the time to remove forms and begin carving. Because the piece isn't completely hard, it's important not to shock the piece with hard impacts. The first three days will be ideal for carving. Keep the surface damp to prevent dust. Surface finishes and textures can be carried out on the ever-hardening casting. Different forming techniques will require that the bleeding evaporates, or that the piece has reached a level of firmness before proceeding. Professional finishers learn to understand and work with the consistencies and set points of concrete to achieve a range of desired effects. Keep notes on the consistencies of your mixes, and time set points for your work conditions to serve you as a guide for future projects.

Curing Concrete

At the end of a work session or the completion of a technique, you'll want your concrete to cure—to be allowed to complete the hydration process with the necessary amount of moisture to create a strong piece. Figure 2 diagrams the rate of the curing process.

As you can see, the first week is when most of the strength in the material is achieved; however, the process continues essentially throughout the

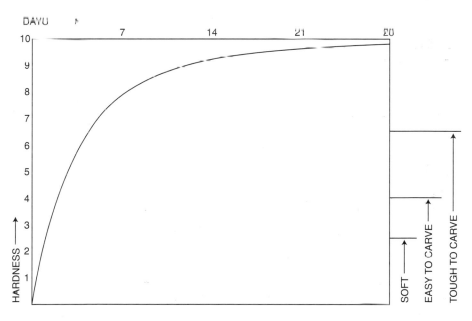
Figure 2: Concrete cure chart

life of the concrete form. Have you ever tried to drill into an old concrete block and thought that they must have made them harder back then? Not so; the block has just continued to harden through the hydration process.

To cure your concrete project, keep the following instructions in mind:
1. Keep the piece moist for a minimum of three to five days.
2. Cover the piece completely in plastic (large plastic garbage bags or 2 mil dropclothes work well).
3. If possible, keep out of direct sunlight and strong wind.

Another method is to soak sections of newspapers or burlap bags in water and then wrap the piece. This process may cause slight discoloration to the surface. If you're concerned about surface texture or discoloration of a piece, you can leave it unwrapped, taking care to mist it with water three or four times a day for the required time. You might even choose to submerge a small piece in a bucket of water to cure. Duration of curing times and any variations to the above-mentioned techniques will be noted in the projects' instructions.

Cleaning Concrete

There may be instances when you need to clean a concrete surface or clean materials you're using in conjunction with concrete that have residue on them. Embedded materials used in certain surface treatments are a good example. Your first line of defense is to work as cleanly as you can, wiping areas with a slightly damp sponge to remove surface debris. However, that may not always be completely effective. Ease of cleanup also depends on the type of materials you're embedding. Glass or glazed materials clean up easily, while porous unglazed ceramic or organic materials, such as rocks and shells, can be more difficult.

First, try to clean the surface of your embedded materials within 12 or 24 hours of your initial work period by scrubbing with plain water and a little elbow grease. You want to wait until the concrete surface is firmly set and won't be marred by your cleaning, but not so long that the piece has already hardened. The best tools to use for cleaning are a small,

stiff nylon brush, such as a nailbrush; an old toothbrush; a white scrubbing pad that in the tile-setting trade is called a "doodle bug" (sorry, I don't know why); a craft cream stick (to pry off any wayward chunks of material without scratching the glazed surface); and, as a final resort, a stainless-steel brush about the size of a toothbrush. Use water as you're cleaning, and rinse thoroughly when you're finished so that the residue doesn't dry back onto the surface. You'll be amazed how clean the surfaces can get.

The next approach is to use chemicals—muriatic acid or sulfamic acid. Note that both have "acid" in their names. These materials have to be used with the utmost care. In addition to the suggested use included here, thoroughly read any instructions that come with the materials, and when working with them, always err on the side of safety.

When working with these chemicals I always wear long pants and shirt sleeves, close-toed shoes and socks, rubber gloves, goggles, and a safety mask. If I'm cleaning a large piece, I may even wear a face shield and a cap. Work in an area with good ventilation, preferably outdoors, with a hose nearby. As an added precaution, don't work near your car. In rare situations, fumes from the muriatic acid can actually damage the paint job. Also, make sure that all pets and children *stay away* while you're using these materials.

MURIATIC ACID

Muriatic acid is found in the concrete area or in the swimming pool section of home improvement centers. It's commonly used to balance the pH of pool water.

Use a plastic container for mixing, and wear gloves and goggles. It won't take much solution to clean an average-sized piece, and you don't want to have too much unused material to dispose of when you're finished. Mix one or two cups (.24 or .48 L) at a time. Always put your measure of water in the container first, and then add the acid. Don't lean directly over the bottle as you open the muriatic acid. Once you open it, you'll notice steamlike fumes coming out of the bottle that you don't want to inhale. Mix a 1 to 5 solution: 1 part acid to 5 parts water. If you brush the solution onto the concrete, you'll see some fizzing. That shows that the solution is working.

Spray the piece you're working on with water. Focus on cleaning any embedded materials by brushing on the solution and then scrubbing it using the same tools listed above. Rinse periodically to neutralize the solution and to rinse the debris so that it doesn't dry back onto the surface. Again, you'll see that glass surfaces clean easily, while organic ones require more work or additional applications of the acid. When you've finished cleaning the surface treatment, use a large scrub brush to go lightly over the entire surface of the piece to even out the surface color and remove streaking that may have occurred with the acid. Rinse liberally, including the bottom and interior space.

SULFAMIC ACID

Sulfamic acid comes in a dry crystal form and is usually found in the tile section of your home improvement center. Two to three ounces (60 to 90 mL) in 1 gallon (3.8 L) of warm water will provide a solution that will clean off a light haze. This chemical doesn't have the same hazardous fumes as muriatic acid, but still needs to be handled with extreme caution.

When I'm finished, I pour the remaining acid solution into a 5-gallon (19 L) bucket of water to dilute it further before disposing of safely. I then use the hose to rinse the area where I was cleaning. I also rinse the tools, gloves, and goggles thoroughly.

Virginia Bullman and LaNelle Davis, *Otha, the Chicken Lady*, 1999, Funky Chicken Art Project, Dahlonega, GA. approx. 5 feet tall (1.5 m). Cement formed over chicken wire armature; adorned with broken dishes. Photo by Hank Margeson

Custom Recipes

Most of the projects can be constructed with premixes, but as you explore concrete as a creative medium, you may want to try working with custom mixes. Here are some recommendations from a variety of sources that have had good results. Through trial and error, you might come up with your own personal favorite. The cement used in these recipes can be gray or white portland, type I. The sand (silica) can be masonry, play, or marble. Each recipe is referred to by number in the project instructions in Chapter 4.

1
Basic Concrete Mix

This is the basic mix that's used for most utilitarian purposes. The gravel provides an inexpensive bulk and added strength. It's ideal for footings or permanent installations. Due to the size of the gravel in the mix, 1/4 inch to 1 inch (6 mm to 2.5 cm), you won't use it too often for the projects.

   1 part cement
   2 parts sand
   3 parts gravel
Approximately 1/2 part water
Add just enough water so that all the particles are well coated with cement paste and the mix is not crumbly.

2
Decorative Aggregate

This is a variation on the Basic Concrete Mix, however, the decorative gravel will more often be in the 1/4-inch (6 mm) or smaller size range. An assortment of aggregates can be used to create a decorative surface that is exposed once the surface concrete is washed off. The resulting surface is a favorite in residential projects, such as driveways and patios, but has been adapted in Chapter 4 for use with smaller projects.

   1 part cement
   2 parts sand
   3 parts decorative gravel, such as river rock, marble chips, or colored aquarium gravel
Approximately 1/2 part water

3
Basic Sand Mix

This versatile mix works well for many of the projects. It's good for casting stepping-stones or for modeling. The consistency of the mix will alter slightly based on how you'll be using the mixture. Adjust your water amount carefully.

   1 part cement
   3 parts sand
   Approximately 1/2 part water

4
Fine Sand Mix

When carving, you don't want your tool to catch on a small rock that could scratch the surface or leave a hole. The key to this mix is sifting your dry ingredients. Most of the time, you'll want to add enough water to end up with a consistency that resembles muffin batter.

   1 part cement
   3 parts sifted sand*
   Approximately 1/2 part water
* If substituting a dry premix for this recipe, sift the bagged ingredients before mixing.

5
Super Sand Mix

This mix could be used instead of the Basic Sand Mix. The consideration here is that, with the addition of the air-entraining agents, it's necessary to use a power mixer.

   1 part cement
   2 to 3 parts sand
   Poly fibers (polyester or polypropylene)
   1 teaspoon (5 mL) air entraining agent
   Approximately 1/2 part water or polymer admix
This is best used as a first application. The poly fibers make the surface look fuzzy, but they can be burned off.

6
Mortar Mix

A sand mix can be used as mortar, but the true mortar mix includes hydrated lime, which makes the mix creamier in texture and easy to work with in various masonry projects. This mix is also used as a stucco coat, with or without color added. Aim for the muffin batter consistency—stiff enough not to drip, but sticky enough to stick.

1 part cement
1/4 to 1 1/4 parts hydrated lime
3 to 6 parts sand
Approximately 1/2 to 1 part water

7
Hypertufa Mix

Polypropylene fibers have been added to this mix to help reduce shrinkage cracks and to add tensile strength. If you use a 1 gallon (3.8 L) container as your "part" measurement, 1/3 cup (.1 L) of fibers, lightly packed, straight out of the bag, is recommended. Separate the fibers before adding them to the mix or they will remain in clumps.

1 part cement
1 1/2 parts peat moss*
1 1/2 parts perlite*
Polypropylene fibers
Water
* Plain potting soil, without fertilizers, can be substituted for the peat moss/perlite combination.

8
Vermiculite Carving Mix

Add the water slowly as you combine it with the dry ingredients so that the lightweight vermiculite won't separate and float to the top. When the mixture is creamy and about the consistency of mayonnaise, you're ready to cast your forms for carving.

1 part cement
2 parts vermiculite
Approximately 1 part water
Variation: replace the cement and vermiculite with white portland and perlite.

9
Polyadam Concrete System Neat Mix

The fabrication methods of the Polyadam Concrete System begin with this Neat Mix. The water initiates the chemical reaction that adds strength to this mix, but don't add any more initially or later.

3 parts cement
1 part PII
1/4 part water, no more
*See page 143 for ordering information

10
Polyadam Concrete System Basic Mix

You start with the Neat Mix and then add your silica (sand) aggregate.

3 parts cement
3 parts sand (can vary amount of sand up to 4 parts)
1 part PII
1/4 part water, no more
*See page 143 for ordering information

11
Fiber Cement

The materials are mixed to a clay-like consistency that are responsive to sculptural forming techniques. Experiment with these ingredients to create your own ideal mix to use to build over armatures.

White portland cement
Stainless-steel wool
Latex polymer (an emulsion that is 70-percent water)
Silica fume
Super plasticizer

12
Finish-Coat Fiber Cement

This mixture is applied over the above Fiber Cement. After you have mixed your ingredients, fold in colored pigments to create lines of colors that will be accentuated in the final polishing. Once again, experimentation is the key to developing a successful mix.

White portland cement
Carbon fibers
Latex polymer (an emulsion that is 70-percent water)
White metakaolin
Super plasticizers

13
Polymer Admix

Any mix can be made stronger with the addition of latex or acrylic polymers. Combine the two ingredients, and substitute the liquid for the plain water in your mixes.

1 part polymer
4 parts water

SLURRY

When you add layers of concrete to a form, there are two things you can do to help provide the strongest bond possible. First, make sure that the form is damp so it will not pull moisture from the material you're adding, and two, apply a binder or cement slurry.

Slurry is cement mixed with a liquid to a consistency similar to ranch dressing. When I mix a batch for a medium-sized project, such as a birdbath, I'll use an 8-ounce (28 g) plastic container as my measuring unit and mix the slurry in a 1-pound (.45 kg) plastic food container. This will usually be plenty for a good work session.

14
Basic Slurry Mix
2 parts cement
1 part water

15
Fortified Slurry Mix
2 parts cement
1 part polymer admix or straight latex polymer

16
PII Slurry
I use this slurry on my polystyrene foam forms when I apply the Polyadam Concrete System.
1 part cement
1 part PII
¼ part water, no more
*See page 143 for ordering information

Virginia Bullman and LaNelle Davis, *Hands Open*, 1999, Lightning Brown memorial bench public installation on the city's greenway in Chapel Hill, NC. Approximately 5 x 4 feet (1.5 x 1.2 m) high, 36 inches (91.4 cm) deep. Hypertufa concrete mix of portland cement, peat moss, and vermiculite applied over a steel rebar armature shaped with wire mesh. Photo by Seth Tice-Lewis

Forming & Construction Techniques

The type of piece you design will dictate the techniques you'll want to consider for its construction. Extended arms on a figure or a sweeping, abstract, arched form will require the additional support of an armature rather than being carved out of solid concrete. If your design for a carving is based on a cylinder, cast a cylindrical form first, then modify it with carving. An animal sculpture could be directly modeled, or it could be cast from a more sophisticated piece mold. The goal is to choose a technique that best enhances your idea.

The following processes provide a wide range of easy forming methods. In addition to the projects included in Chapter 4, an understanding of these techniques will allow you to develop more individualized explorations as you continue to work with concrete.

Simple Casting

Simple casting techniques can be used to create functional or artistic items such as planters, bowls, masks, sculptures, decorative plaques, or stepping stones. With a basic understanding of the process, you can experiment with the complexity and scale of your molds. I have a personal approach to any new technique: start small and simple. This allows you to understand the princi-

Jack Hastings, *Fountain-El Presidio Plaza*, 1970, Tucson, AZ. 14 x 4 feet (4.2 x 1.2 m). Carved cement. Photo by artist

ples and materials without wasting time, energy, or supplies. Of course, there are those times when we feel the need to jump in to make a larger-than-life statement and manage to do so successfully. If that's how you approach things—go for it!

Casting is basically pouring or compressing a material that's in a somewhat liquid state into a confined shape or mold and allowing that material to set or become hard, so that when the mold is removed, the material has assumed that shape. Another way to think of it is that when a material is poured or compressed into a *negative* or hollow form (the mold) and allowed to set, once the mold is removed, the *positive* of that form now exists. You need to have a negative to create the finished positive.

SELECTING A MOLD

The term *mold* is usually used in reference to a structure that will produce the same likeness each time. A *form* is used to cast a mass of an approximate shape and size. A variety of materials can be used to create molds and forms, including plastic, rubber, wood, metal, plaster, and sand. The technology can be quite refined, enabling you to cast detailed likenesses and complex forms. It can also be as simple as items found around the home or shop. For the purposes of this book, I'm going to concentrate on the latter.

Regardless of the material selected to make your mold, there's one impor-

Various molds, clockwise from bottom left: commercial plastic stepping stone mold, large coffee can, homemade wooden mold, plastic waste can, Venetian Bench top mold, polystyrene core, metal form, plastic planter liner. Center: Venetian Bench base mold (see page 130)

tant question to consider: when you finish your casting, how are you going to get the hardened concrete out of the mold? It's not as silly or simplistic a consideration as you might think. Some mold materials are flexible and can be peeled off the hardened casting. Rigid molds constructed from a softer material, such as plaster or polystyrene foam, are used only once and then chipped or broken away to reveal the permanent piece. These molds are commonly called *waste molds*.

If there's an undercut in the form you want to cast—a bulge or depression that would get caught in a single mold piece, such as an ear on a cast human head—it may be necessary to create a multipiece mold from rigid materials, such as plaster or fiberglass. This type of mold, a *piece mold*, can be taken apart after each casting to produce the permanent piece. The sections are then

reassembled and used for subsequent castings. A well-designed and constructed mold can be a thing of beauty in its own right.

Plastic Molds

Plastic shapes make great molds. Some garden centers or craft stores have commercially produced molds available to create stepping-stones or garden pathways. However, don't overlook the culinary departments when searching for interesting shapes to cast. Cake pans, take-out containers, and other food molds can easily be adapted for creative castings.

Wood Molds

If you want square molds or any variation of angular geometry, wood enables you to construct limitless variations to suit your needs. Keep in mind that the larger the mold you're building, the more likely that the wooden sides will need to be reinforced or supported. Consider this:

the larger your form, the more concrete it will take to fill; the more concrete you pour into that form, the more pressure there will be on the sides of your form by the sheer volume of concrete. That pressure will push out and curve any unsupported sections of wood. Instead of being crisp and square, the shape will more closely resemble an overstuffed pillow. See pages 93 and 97 for examples of wood molds and the supports used to prevent expansion of the concrete.

Metal Molds

Aluminum roof flashing can be cut into strips and fashioned into curved shapes; however, the aluminum is not rigid enough to hold those shapes once they're filled with concrete. When you build a metal mold, you'll need to support the strips with a wood or polystyrene foam framework (see figure 1).

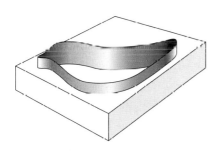

Figure 1

PREPARING THE MOLD

Concrete will stick to some types of mold materials more than others. To avoid this, you should always use a releasing agent. Commercially produced mold releases are available, but a number of other items also work well. Some that I've found

effective are diesel fuel, motor oil, petroleum jelly, spray lubricants, and non-flavored cooking sprays.

When preparing a mold, you want to apply an even coat of lubricant so that the whole surface appears shiny, without drips, puddles, or large deposits. I prefer to brush on diesel fuel or motor oil, or rub petroleum jelly onto a wooden mold because wood tends to be more absorbent than other mold materials. For plastic or metal, a light coating of a spray lubricant works great. You'll need to pay particular attention to corners or details when applying any releasing agent to a mold.

REINFORCING THE CASTING

Unless you're casting small objects, you'll want to add some type of reinforcement to your piece. The reinforcing material will add strength and integrity to the piece, and if a concrete piece develops a crack, the reinforcing material will hold sections together until repairs can be made.

The type of material you'll select for reinforcing will depend on the size of the project you're working on. A stepping-stone might use a piece of $1/2$-inch (1.3 cm) galvanized hardware cloth, while a section of garden wall would require a grid of $1/2$-inch (1.3 cm) rebar. Another consideration when selecting a reinforcing material is that the largest aggregate used in your concrete mix should be able to easily pass through the spaces in the reinforcement. In other words, the

aggregate needs to be able to pass through the mesh you use.

You should plan and prepare your reinforcing material so it's ready to use before you mix the concrete. In some cases, you'll simply insert the reinforcing material midway through the casting process. In other instances, those elements will be preformed and suspended in the mold. If you're cutting hardware cloth or some other type of metal mesh to lay in a mold, be sure the mesh is smaller than the mold. If the reinforcing materials touch or protrude onto the sides of the mold, it may make it difficult when you try to remove the cast piece from the mold, even causing the piece to break.

CASTING A SIMPLE MOLD OR FORM

As you prepare your work area, take into account the logistics of casting. Will it be easy to physically pour the concrete into the mold? Is the mold on a surface that you can move or turn if needed? If you're working outside, will the weather cooperate? Will you be working in a shaded area? Each of the casting projects in Chapter 4 will detail how to construct or find the mold needed. Once you've selected your mold, follow these instructions.

Materials and Tools

CONCRETE MIX: Premixed Sand (Topping) Mix, Masonry Mix, or Mix 3
— Plastic, wood, or metal mold, either purchased, found, or constructed

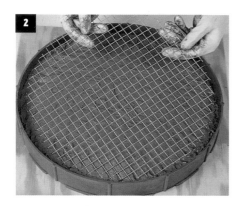

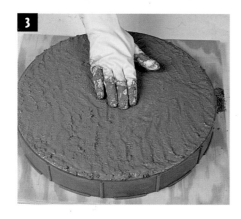

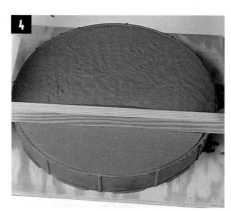

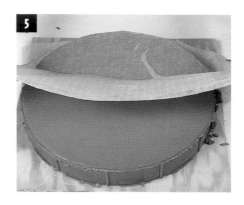

— 4 mil plastic to cover work area and work boards
— 2 work boards: one to cast on, and one to turn over the casting when finished
— Mold release agent
— Reinforcing material: ½-inch (1.3 cm) hardware cloth
— Aviator shears
— Container to mix concrete
— Screed
— Paper or synthetic towels (optional)
— Putty knife
— Sponge
— Water container
— File (optional)

Instructions

1
Cover the work area and board with plastic.

2
Construct or select your mold.

3
Apply the selected mold release lubricant to the inside of the mold (photo 1).

4
With the aviator shears, cut the hardware cloth ½-inch (1.3 cm) smaller than the inside of the mold and set aside.

5
Mix enough concrete to fill the mold.

6
As you begin to cast, take your time, and make sure that all of the corners and edges are filled. Fill the mold halfway.

7
Position the hardware cloth in the mold so that it doesn't touch the sides of the mold (photo 2).

8
Continue to fill the mold until the concrete brims (photo 3).

9
To achieve a strong casting, you want to eliminate large air bubbles, and you do this through agitation. Small molds placed on a work board can be agitated by picking up a corner of the board and tapping it up and down against the table surface. Some molds may require tapping on the side with a hammer. A small electric sander held onto the side of a mold can also create enough of a vibration to cause air bubbles to rise to the surface.

10

Screed or level off the top of the mold (photo 4). To do this effectively, position the straightedge board you're using as you screed across the back edge of the mold. Move it in a side-to-side sawing motion as you move the board toward you. Don't clean off your work board after screeding. The excess material around your mold actually works as a dam to stop additional concrete from seeping out of the mold. Later, you may even need a little of that concrete to finish off your piece.

11

Allow any bleeding, or water that has accumulated on the surface, to evaporate. You can also lay sheets of paper or synthetic towels on top of the casting to absorb some of the excess water (photo 5). Repeat if more water collects.

12

Allow the casting to remain undisturbed for five to six hours (if it's a small mold, say the size of a stepping stone) or until the concrete feels firm and no water shows when you rub your finger back and forth over the surface.

13

Clean your work board of excess concrete. If you've made a reverse-cast mosaic (like the example used here), reserve this material to finish your piece, and follow steps 13 and 16 for Reverse-Cast Mosaics on pages 74 and 75. Clean off any concrete that might be on the edges of the mold by using a plastic putty knife

or a sponge. This will help eliminate chipping when the mold is removed.

14

Remove the mold (photo 6). See the following instructions.

15

Cover the casting with plastic, and leave undisturbed for 24 hours. The casting will be significantly harder after this period.

16

File the edges of the casting if needed.

17

Cure the casting.

REMOVING A MOLD

A small casting, such as a stepping-stone, can be removed from a wood or plastic mold after about six hours. There are no (excuse the pun) hard and fast rules. A more complex mold may need to set up for a day or two. If you continue to work in the medium, you'll develop a certain feel for it, but five to six hours is generally safe. Factors that can vary the time include the amount of water in the concrete mix, humidity, and temperature. The curing process is a chemical one, but those factors contribute to the speed at which it occurs.

A mold that is flexible can be worked gently until they're free from the cast surface. Then they can be lifted off. For other materials, remove any hardware, screws, clamps, or bindings that hold the mold together. Then carefully pull sections away from the casting.

The concrete will not have reached full strength, and may, in fact, be quite fragile. Edges may be vulnerable, so take care at this stage.

POLYSTYRENE FOAM WASTE MOLD

A waste mold is one that's constructed for a single use. The mold is destroyed when the piece is removed. There are several variations of the polystyrene foam waste mold; many can be made with the 1- or 2-inch (2.5 or 5.1 cm) insulation foam (also known as beadboard) that you can find at your home improvement center. Polystyrene foam is so easy to find and inexpensive that it's an ideal material to experiment with.

Materials and Tools

CONCRETE MIX: Premixed Sand (Topping) Mix, Mortar Mix, or Mix 2 or 3
— Polystyrene foam insulation
— Tool to cut polystyrene foam
— 3-inch (7.6 cm) nails
— Double-sided carpet tape (optional)
— Permanent marker
— Drywall compound (optional)
— Aluminum roof flashing (optional)
— Spray lubricant (optional)
— Duct tape
— 4 mil plastic
— Nylon scrub brush

Instructions

1

Design the shape you want to make your cast form.

2

Cut out a paper pattern.

3

Cut a section of polystyrene foam insulation large enough so that it's at least 1 inch (2.5 cm) larger than the pattern all the way around. Cut as many pieces of the insulation as it takes to form the desired thickness of your design.

4

Pin the sections of polystyrene together with 3-inch (7.6 cm) nails. Double-stick carpet tape can also be used to keep the sections together.

5

Position the pattern on the center of the polystyrene foam, and trace it onto the surface with the marker.

6

Cut out the shape through all thicknesses of the polystyrene, entering and exiting through the same cut so that the perimeter of the section stays intact. If the cutout of your polystyrene foam is rougher than you want, you can apply drywall compound to the surface to smooth it. Let it dry and sand lightly, if needed, before casting. No mold release agent is needed for this mold. You can also cut strips of aluminum roof flashing and tape them to fit the contour of the opening (see Figure 1 on page 33). The flashing can be tacked to the sides of the shape with short pieces of the double-stick carpet tape. When the mold is filled with concrete, the metal will hold tight against the sides. Spray the metal with a light coating of spray lubricant.

7

Secure the layers and edges of the mold with duct tape before casting.

8

Lay the mold on a flat, plastic-covered surface to cast.

9

Refer to Chapter 2: Cast a Simple Mold or Form, pages 33 through 35, and follow steps 4 through 9.

10

Trowel the top surface flat.

11

Cover with plastic and allow to sit undisturbed for 24 hours.

12

To remove the mold, take out the nails, break away, and discard the polystyrene foam.

13

Take the casting outside and spray with water. Scrub the surface with the nylon brush to remove any debris.

14

Cover with plastic and cure for one week.

ADAPTING A POLYSTYRENE FOAM WASTE MOLD FOR A TOTEM CONSTRUCTION

Here's a simple variation of the waste-mold technique that will let you stack pieces on a pole to create wonderful totems for the garden.

Bird element cast in a polystyrene foam waste mold with a decorative aggregate (aquarium gravel) surface

Additional Materials and Tools

CONCRETE MIX: Premixed Sand (Topping) Mix, Mortar Mix, or Mix 3
— PVC pipe
— Small wire brush or riffler rasp
— Scissors or tin snips (optional)
— Handsaw
— File

Instructions

1

Follow steps 1 through 6 as explained on pages 35 and 36.

2

Cut a piece of PVC pipe that extends 2 inches (5.1 cm) beyond the polystyrene foam cutout, when the pipe's positioned in the direction you want it to sit on the totem.

3

Unpin sections of polystyrene so that the inside halves are facing up (photo 7).

4

Refer to the instructions for Adapting a Polystyrene Foam Core for a Totem Construction, pages 49 through 50. Proceed, making this significant modification: instead of inserting the pipe into the core, you'll be inserting it into the waste mold. The mold will hold it in position for casting so that it can be incorporated into the final shape (photo 8).

If you have lined your mold with the roof flashing, cut holes at the appropriate locations with the tin snips so the pipe can be positioned.

5

Prepare your hardware cloth by cutting two shapes ½ inch (1.3 cm)

smaller than the inside of your mold.

6

Mix the concrete.

7

Position the waste mold on a plastic-covered work board.

8

Fill the mold with 1 inch (2.5 cm) of concrete. Cut one of the hardware cloth pieces in half and position onto the cast concrete, under the pipe.

9

Continue to fill the mold over the pipe, within 1 inch (2.5 cm) of the top of the mold. Lay the other hardware cloth piece on top of the concrete.

10

Follow steps 9 through 14 from the Polystyrene Waste Mold instructions, page 36.

11

Use the saw to trim the pipe even with the casting. Saw the pipe as close as you can without damaging the piece. File the pipe flush.

SAND CASTING

Sand casting is one of the easiest and most economical ways to get started with casting a variety of shapes or forms. You can create decorative wall hangings, plaques, or picture frames simply by casting concrete into indented shapes in sand. Variations on the Sand-Cast Bowl technique below can produce everything from birdbaths and fountain bowls to masks and planters.

Materials and Tools

CONCRETE MIX: Premixed Sand (Topping) Mix, Mortar Mix or Mix 3; Slurry Mix 14
concrete
- 4 mil plastic
- 2 gallons (7.6 L) sand
- Water
- Dry-cleaning plastic bag
  Permanent marker (optional)
- Aviator shears
- Reinforcing material
- Container to mix concrete
- Putty knife
- Large plastic trash bag
- Milk crate
- Coarse rasp or file

Instructions

1

Cover a sturdy worktable with 4 mL plastic.

2

Place approximately 1½ gallons (5.7 L) of the sand toward the middle of your work area so that your finished form will be at least 4 inches (10.2 cm) from any edge of the table.

3

Mix enough water into the sand so that it packs easily (photo 9). Remember the last time you made a sand castle at the beach? That's the consistency you're looking for.

4

Form a shape on the table that will be the inside shape you want for your bowl (photo 10). You're working in reverse, casting the bowl upside down. The height of your mound will be the depth of your bowl. Remember, your bowl doesn't need to be round; experiment with the contour of your mound by adding and subtracting the amount of sand. Be sure to pack your sand shape firmly so it won't collapse when you apply the concrete.

5

Clean off excess sand and dry the surrounding plastic. At this point, you might want to use the permanent marker to draw a line on the plastic to define the shape you want for the outside rim or lip of the bowl; it can be a completely different shape than your sand mound or guide. This line can also serve as a pattern for cutting your reinforcing material.

6

Cover the sand form with a single layer of dry-cleaning plastic. Allow the edge of the dry-cleaning plastic to extend several inches past your mound (photo 11). If you want to end up with a sandy texture on your bowl, don't use the dry-cleaning plastic; cast directly on the sand. Casting on the plastic results in a slick, smooth surface.

7

Cut the reinforcing material with the aviator shears to the shape and size of the finished bowl. Your reinforcing materials will be larger than the sand form, but not larger than the finished bowl.

8

Mix the concrete. Take a handful of concrete and form it into a ³/₄-inch-thick (1.9 cm) "hamburger patty." Lay the patty in the middle of your form (photo 12).

9

Make another patty, and place it so that it overlaps the first by at least ½ inch (1.3 cm). Pat lightly until the seam line disappears (photo 13).

10

Continue applying the concrete in this manner until the form is covered to an even thickness of approximately ½ inch (1.3 cm). Notice that in this

instance, the actual look of the bowl differs from the original sand-cast form.

11

Use the putty knife to trim the concrete to refine the finished shape.

12

Place the reinforcing material over the concrete and press in lightly to embed (photo 14). You may need to add a small amount of concrete over the surface to secure the material to the bowl form (photo 15). Don't worry if some of the hardware cloth shows through.

13

Pull the edges of the dry-cleaning plastic toward the center of the casting (photo 16). This will help you coax the concrete back (these things have a way of growing as you work), and compress the material at the edge, making it stronger. Leave the plastic in the drawn-up position.

14

Cover the piece with an unopened trash bag, and leave undisturbed overnight.

15

The next morning, remove the trash bag and pull back the dry-cleaning plastic.

16

Open up the trash bag, and use it to line the inside of the milk crate.

17

Carefully pick up the rim of your bowl, and lift it off of the sand. It's easier to pick up the rim if you put one hand under the plastic that's covering the table. Lift the bowl from underneath, and grab the rim with the other hand (photo 17).

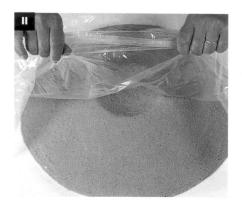

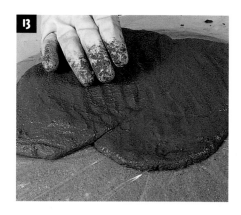

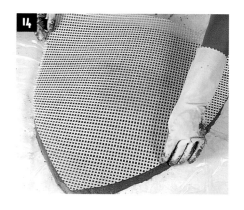

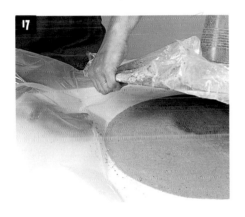

18
Place the bowl right side up in the milk crate. File any thin areas, and define the shape as needed.

19
Spray the bowl with water, and secure the plastic bag around it. Remove the sand from your worktable.

20
The instructions for the cast bowl, with or without the connector (see the following instructions), are for creating a base form. To finish the bowl, you'll want to add more concrete to the surface to add strength and refine it. Refer to Chapter 3: Surface Treatments to explore your options.

Larger versions of this technique have even been utilized to create architectural structures. Instead of sand, large dirt mounds are formed, a reinforcing structure is constructed, and the concrete is applied. When hardened, the dirt is dug out to reveal an interior space.

BOWL CONNECTOR

For some of your constructions, such as the Birdbath on page 100, you'll want to add a stem to the bottom of the bowl so that you can connect it to a base. A plastic drinking cup provides a simple and effective means of creating a connecting system.

Additional Materials and Tools
— 16-ounce (480 mL) plastic cup
— Utility knife
— Needle-nose pliers

Instructions

1
Cast your bowl following the Sand Casting instructions, pages 37 through 39, up through step 12.

2
Determine where the center of balance of the bowl is located, and make a mark in the wet concrete.

Kem Alexander, *Richard and the Mrs.*, 2000, 11.5 x 2 inches (29.2 x 5.1 cm). Masonry with ceramic plate and metal; hand-formed using a bowl mold with a wire infrastructure. Photo by artist

3

Fill the cup with concrete, agitating it as you go, to avoid air bubbles. Fill the cup completely, and then add a little more so that it resembles a glass of soda when the foam crests slightly above the rim of the glass.

4

Turn the cup over, and place it at the marked point. Give the cup a gentle twist. Eye it from several angles so you're sure it's straight, and then leave the cup in place (photo 18). Follow steps 13 through 17 on page 38.

5

With the utility knife, carefully score the plastic cup. Use the needle-nose pliers to grab and remove the cup (photo 19). Continue with steps 18 through 20 on pages 38 and 39 to complete your form.

Forming Armatures

An armature is the skeleton of a sculpture—the inner support. Often, when building a sculpture, we want heavy materials to move upward and soft materials to move outward. The armature is the framework we build on to make that possible.

When you're creating a sculptural form, you need to think about the piece from the inside out. While you don't want to know exactly what the piece will look like when completed (after all, the joy of creating is the process of discovery!), you need to make some plans for the direction the piece will take.

As a "skeleton," the armature needs to be contained within the piece; it must be smaller in volume than your vision of the completed piece. A bulky armature will only get bulkier as you apply the materials to it.

By its nature, concrete is heavy, but your choice of armature material can help you minimize the weight of your completed form. An armature utilizing a cardboard tube creates air space; a piece of polystyrene foam that fills the center of your form will help lighten the construction. While your finished piece doesn't have to be solid concrete to be substantial; however, the type of material you select for your armature should be consistent with the scale of the work.

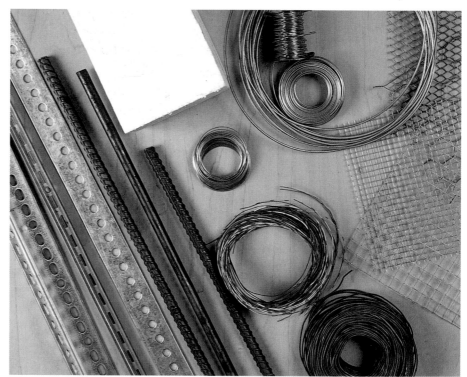

Materials for armature forming, clockwise from top left: polystyrene foam, galvanized clothesline wire, stainless steel wire, galvanized wire, expanded galvanized metal mesh, chicken wire, ¼ inch (6 mm) hardware cloth, ½ inch (1.3 cm) hardware cloth, tire wire, rebar, steel rod, slotted metal shelf brackets. Center: small roll of galvanized wire, larger roll of plastic-coated copper wire (telephone wire)

SIMPLE COLUMN ARMATURE

Modified versions of this construction technique can produce pedestal stands for birdbaths, fountains, or gazing balls. Pushed further, figurative forms can easily be developed. The actual armature in this construction is the layered hardware cloth. The purpose of the tube is to act as a barrier for the concrete to be compressed against as it's worked through the mesh. If not for the tube, the concrete would fill the column, making it a much heavier piece than necessary.

Materials and Tools

CONCRETE MIX: Premixed Sand (Topping) Mix, Mortar Mix, or Mix 3; Slurry Mix 14
— Cardboard or plastic tube
— Tape measure
— Aviator shears
— Reinforcing material: ½-inch (1.3 cm) hardware cloth
— Angle wire cutters
— 6-inch (15.2 cm) pieces of 22-gauge wire
— Leather work gloves
— Chicken wire
— Hammer
— Container to mix concrete
— Plastic trash bags
— Putty knife with tooth-shaped blade
— File or rasp

Instructions

1
Select the size tube you want to use as a core to form your armature. For most of the project examples, I recommend tubes 4 inches (10.2 cm) in diameter.

2
Determine the size of the piece of hardware cloth you'll need to wrap the tube. First measure the length of the tube. This is the height measurement of your hardware cloth. The length is 2¼ times the circumference of your tube. You want to be able to wrap the mesh around the tube twice with an overlapping edge (photo 20).

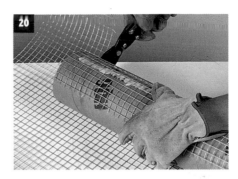

3
Roll the hardware cloth tightly around the tube, and secure it with several pieces of wire (photo 21).

4
Continue to add wires every 3 inches (7.6 cm) or so to ensure that the overlapping edge lies flat.

5
The foot or base of the column is the flared shape at the bottom that provides weight and area to enable the column to stand. The taller the column, the larger or heavier the base should be to counterbalance the height. The foot or base is formed with a roll of chicken wire. Use a piece of chicken wire 15 x 30 inches (38.1 x 76.2 cm) for a 4-inch (10.2 cm) tube. Lay the chicken wire so that the twisted elements are perpendicular to your body, and roll it over itself (photo 22).

6
Compress the chicken wire tube into a donut shape with a hole the same size as the diameter of the tube (photo 23).

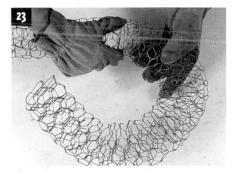

7
Place it around the bottom of the tube, and use a few pieces of wire to attach it to the hardware cloth (photo 24).

8
Use the hammer to tap the chicken wire so it doesn't stick up too high; coax it into shape.

9
Lay out an unopened trash bag on the floor and place the column armature in the middle.

10
Mix the concrete. Apply the concrete in small handfuls, working it through the mesh as if you were grating cheese through a grater (photo 25).

11
Continue doing this until the hardware cloth is covered (some of the mesh may be visible on the surface; this is not a problem for a first application) and the chicken wire base is filled with concrete (photo 26).

12
To facilitate additional applications of concrete, use the tooth-shaped putty knife to texture the column surface (photo 27). This is like a scratch coat in the stucco process; the ridges provide a rough surface for the next layer to grip onto.

13
When finished, clean off any concrete that may have dropped, pull the edges of the trash bag over the base, and slide another trash bag over the column to completely cover. Leave until the next day.

14
When you return, uncover the column. File any thin areas and refine the base shape as needed (photo 28).

15
With the above steps, you have created a base form. You'll want to add more concrete or reinforcing to strengthen and refine your form. This form can be used to continue with another surface treatment. See Chapter 3 for your options.

In the example shown in photo 25, I included another element. The plastic cup at the top of the column has been incorporated to mold a hollow sleeve at the top of a birdbath base to fit the corresponding stem on the bowl (see instructions on pages 39 through 40). This simple connection can also be utilized for other sculptural constructions.

Additional Materials and Tools
— 16-ounce (480 mL) plastic cup
— Needle-nose pliers

Instructions

1
Select the tube for your armature. Set, don't force, the 16-ounce (480 mL) cup into one end of the tube. If it drops through the hole, the opening will already be large enough to hold the stem connection.

2
If the cup only goes partially into the hole, you need to include the length it extends when you're measuring to determine the height measurement of your hardware cloth.

3
Follow steps 2 through 10 in the previous instructions.

4

When you apply the concrete, take extra care to fill the space between the mesh and the cup so that the material is compressed, but the cup isn't distorted and remains straight. Follow steps 11 through 15.

5

In addition to following step 14, use the needle-nose pliers to remove the plastic cup.

POLYSTYRENE FOAM AS A COLUMN ARMATURE

Another variation of this technique is to construct a shape or form that functions the same way as the tube—acting as an initial support for the mesh and a barrier for the concrete. This is how I formed the Gazing Ball Stand, page 113. A cardboard construction could also be used for this process.

Materials and Tools

CONCRETE MIX: Premixed Sand (Topping) Mix, Mortar Mix, or Mix 3; Slurry Mix 14
— Polystyrene foam
— Wire brushes
— 4 mil plastic
— Duct tape
— Roofing nails
— Paper for pattern
— Scissors
— Leather work gloves
— Expanded galvanized mesh
— 22-gauge wire
— Container to mix concrete
— Plastic trash bags
— Container to mix slurry
— Paintbrush
— Mallet (optional)

Instructions

1

Shape a cone out of the polystyrene foam. See the instructions for Carving a Polystyrene Foam Armature on pages 47 through 49.

2

Cover the foam shape with the 4 mil plastic, and tape all the edges closed with duct tape. Secure the plastic to the foam with roofing nails as needed.

3

Make a paper pattern to use as a template to cut out the sections of expanded mesh. The pattern should conform to the surface, and the edges should butt together.

4

Cut one piece of expanded mesh using the pattern.

5

Wire the edges of the mesh together at the seam (photo 29).

6

Mix the concrete. Apply the concrete using the cheese grater method, rubbing it though the mesh.

7

Cover the armature with a plastic bag and leave overnight.

8

Add about 2 inches (5.1 cm) to one side of the paper pattern, and cut out a second piece of mesh.

9

Mix the slurry and concrete. Wet down the concrete form and apply the slurry.

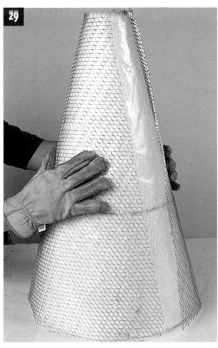

A polystyrene foam cone covered in plastic makes a good core to support wire mesh to compress the concrete against when you want to build a hollow structure.

10

Layer the second piece of mesh onto the form and wire the seam together. Trim if needed so that the edges butt together.

11

Apply the concrete as previously described. Cover and leave overnight.

12

Uncover and remove the polystyrene foam core. It may be necessary to use a mallet to help force the cone out, but with care you'll be able to use the form again.

13

Use this base form to proceed with a selected surface treatment (see Chapter 3).

METAL ARMATURES

Scale will be a significant factor when deciding what material to use to make your armature. Small figures, up to 2 feet (61 cm) high, can be constructed from different gauges of wire, or malleable pipe or tubing. A figure with outstretched arms or legs will need to be constructed carefully to ensure structural support for the extensions. Larger figures can be constructed out of pipes, firmly wired rebar, bolted slotted metal, or even welded metal.

Before you start to construct your armature, think about the form you want to create. How big will it be? How will the weight of the piece be distributed? Where will it touch the ground? What will stick out? A scale sketch can help you plan the amount of materials you'll need to have on hand.

Think in volume as you plan the armature. A human figure isn't a flat paper doll. The torso more closely resembles a rectangle, so you want to have at least four pieces of metal to construct a rectangular form. If the figure is to be standing, you want to be able to support the weight on the legs. Consider using a longer piece of material that begins to form the legs and continues through the figure's torso. The armature is *like* a skeleton, but you don't need to provide all the same joints. The goal is to try to create a rigid construction that still suggests the gesture or indicates the activity or movement. Whether you're constructing a figure or an animal, the principles are the same.

Virginia Bullman and LaNelle Davis, *Laughing Lady*, 1999, approximately 7 feet (2.1 m). Cement formed over chicken wire armature, adorned with broken dishes.
Photo by Seth Tice-Lewis

SIMPLE ANIMAL ARMATURE

The full instructions for this particular animal, including the cut list for the rebar, are found on page 111. Modify the length of the legs and body or the position of the head to form different animals.

Materials and Tools

CONCRETE MIX: Premixed Sand (Topping) Mix, Mortar Mix, Mix 3; Slurry Mix 14
— Leather gloves
— Metal-cutting saw
— Rebar cut to required lengths
— Grinder or file
— Wire cutters
— Tie wire
— Lineman's pliers
— Rusty metal primer
— Galvanized clothesline wire
— 22-gauge wire
— Aviator shears
— Expanded galvanized metal mesh
— Container to mix concrete
— 2 mil plastic
— Rasps or rubbing block
— Container to mix slurry
— Paintbrush

Instructions

1

Design your armature. Cut the rebar to the designated lengths. Cut pieces of tie wire to a comfortable work length, about 18 inches (45.7 cm).

2

Start with the side and leg pieces (see figure 2). Overlap the pieces of rebar so that each piece extends ³/₄ inch (1.9 cm). With the leather gloves on, wrap the wire tightly, and twist to secure. Use the lineman's pliers to make the tightest connection you can (photo 30). Wire both sides.

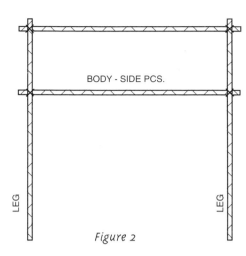

BODY - SIDE PCS.

LEG

LEG

Figure 2

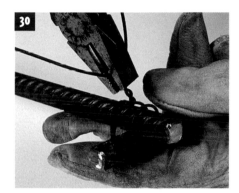

30

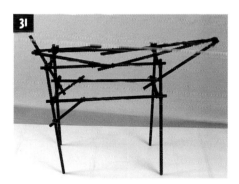

31

32

3
Connect the two sides together with the front and back pieces. At this point, you have a rectangle on legs.

4
Use wire to attach the two pieces of rebar for the top of the head to the body with wire. Add the lower head support by securing it to the top side of the lower front piece. When you're adding pieces to your armature, consider what's the best way a piece can be supported. In this case, by attaching the head support to the top side of the lower front, rather than underneath, the head will be better supported (refer to photo 31).

5
Join the three head pieces together with wire.

6
Wire on the back leg supports on the outside of your armature.

7
Secure the tail support pieces.
Note: If your armature seems a bit wobbly, try to tighten the connections by holding onto one of the wrapped wires with your lineman's pliers and twisting it a half turn. An extra section or two of rebar can be added if you feel it's needed. The form will also become more stable as you secure mesh over the surface.

Virginia Bullman and LaNelle Davis, *Laughing Lady*, 1999, approximately 5 feet (1.5 m). Cement formed over chicken wire armature, adorned with broken dishes. Photo by Seth Tice-Lewis

8
Spray your rebar structure with primer.

9
Bend the clothesline in half, and shape it into a coil for the tail (photo 32).

10
Wrap the coil with 22-gauge wire, first in one direction and then criss-cross back in the opposite direction, as shown in photo 32.

11
Attach the tail coil to the rebar tail support pieces.

Roy Kanwit, *Egg*, 1994, 3 x 6 x 5 feet (1 x 2 x 1.5 m). White portland ferro-cement direct modeled over steel frame. Photo by artist

12

Wearing your leather gloves, cover the armature with sheets of expanded galvanized mesh to create a contoured surface. Secure the mesh to the rebar and to itself with the 22-gauge wire.

13

Once the back of the animal is covered with mesh, fold up a small scrap of mesh to create a little block about 1 x 2 inches (2.5 x 5.1 cm). Check where the tail coil hits the back, and secure this block to the back and the tail so that the coil is secure and slightly elevated above the back surface. **Note:** A spacer like the one described for the tail is necessary when you're creating an armature for a piece that will have two forms touching each other. Without the spacer on the back of the dog, the tail coil would appear to be growing out of the back instead of resting on it. Along the

same lines, imagine that you're making a figure that has its hands on its hips. A length of the forearm will get immersed as you build up the hip area with concrete. Unless you compensate for the addition of material by making the forearm armature extra long, it will appear short in the finished piece.

14

Fold and bend pieces of mesh to create ear shapes, and secure them to the head area.

15

Mix the concrete. To successfully apply concrete to an expanded mesh surface, it's best to use basic masonry tools. I use a steel trowel as a hawk and a pointed trowel. Load a small pile of concrete onto the rectangular tool. Hold it next to the mesh surface. Hold the pointed trowel in the other hand so the back of the tool is facing the mesh. Cut

into the cement, and with a light pushing movement, stroke the tool in an upward motion. Don't push so hard that the material falls through the mesh, and don't go over the area multiple times. Reposition the tool, holding the concrete so that the next application will slightly overlap the first stroke.

16

Continue to work over the surface in this manner for as long as you can utilize both tools.

17

In more difficult areas, like the belly or the chin, pile a small amount of concrete directly onto the back of the pointed trowel, and apply using the same method described in step 15.

18

Use your hands to apply and compress material into small areas, such as the legs or ears. Squeeze concrete into the wire wrapping around the tail.

19

Don't be too concerned if this first application looks rough, or if there are small areas where material has dropped off. Cover with plastic and allow to set up.

20

After 10 to 24 hours, uncover the piece, spray lightly with water, and remove any unwanted chunks.

21

Wrap another crisscrossing layer of wire over the tail form. Refer to photo 32.

22

Mix the slurry and concrete. Lightly brush the slurry over the form, and apply additional concrete to ensure a solid base and to begin to develop your form.

23

Carefully add concrete to the tail form. Cover with plastic and allow to set.

24

After 10 to 24 hours, uncover the piece, spray lightly with water, and remove any unwanted chunks.

25

Consider how you want the surface of your sculpture to look. You may decide to follow the instructions for direct modeling and have the finished form be natural concrete. This surface can be enhanced with a decorative texture, or you may decide to add embedded elements. Refer to Chapter 3: Surface Treatments, for a full range of options.

POLYSTYRENE FOAM ARMATURES

Polystyrene foam can be carved and shaped into a variety of geometric or curvilinear forms. I have more success forming foam that's made up of compressed beads, rather than foam that's expanded. I also look for a dense compression. To find polystyrene foam, look in the phone directory under "Packaging." Or, try to find a building supplier who sells polystyrene foam for boat docks or archery targets. Contoured polystyrene foam shapes are ideal armatures on which to apply a polymer-fortified concrete or fiberglass system (see pages 57 through 60 for a complete description of this process). The layering of the two materials conforms to the shape. Like any other armature that you add material to, the polystyrene foam must be smaller so the finished piece isn't bulky.

CARVING A POLYSTYRENE FOAM ARMATURE

Whether you're carving wood, concrete, or polystyrene foam, the basics of carving still apply, even though the tools are different. Refer to Carving Basics on page 50.

Materials and Tools

- Polystyrene foam
- Permanent marker
- Cutting tools: handsaws, hot knife, hot wire, band saw
- Large common nails
- Assorted wire brushes

Instructions

1

If you've designed your piece to scale either by making a sketch or a

Tools for shaping polystyrene. Top row, left to right: hot knife, wire brush, small wire brush, drywall saw or key hole saw, pruning saw, assorted wire brushes. Bottom row: wire wheel attachment for drill, caulk gun with construction adhesive

model, draw the scale grid onto your polystyrene foam (see figure 3).

2

Use a pattern, or freehand the profile outline of the design for the side view, front view, and, if you're using one, overhead view, onto the scaled block (photo 33).

3

Use your selected tool to cut out the side view (photo 34). Try to cut it so that the scraps remain as intact as possible.

4

Pin the cut scraps back onto the piece with the large nails so that the block once again appears to be

whole, and you can see the drawing on the other end (photo 35).

5

Turn the piece to follow the lines of the front view as you cut the piece again (photo 36).

6

If you're using a third view, pin the scraps together again to reform the original block; make your third set of cuts. When the scraps fall away, you'll have a blocky likeness of your form (photo 37).

7

Additional cuts can be made on the piece as needed (photo 38).

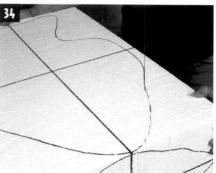

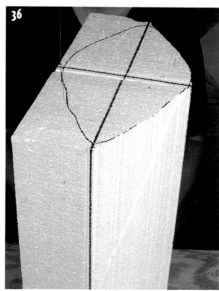

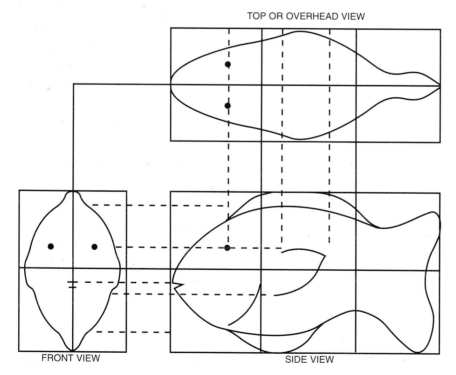

TOP OR OVERHEAD VIEW

FRONT VIEW

SIDE VIEW

Figure 3. A small sketch can be gridded into squares which are then assigned a value so you can enlarge your idea; i.e., 1 inch (2.5 cm) = 6 (15.2 cm) inches. Organizing the way you draw the different views of your sculpture will help you transfer the location of details.

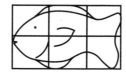

8

You can soften the edges and refine the form with the wire brushes (photo 39).

This basic technique works even for larger pieces. If you don't have a cutting tool available to make the initial profile cuts, your approach will be slightly different and will probably take a little longer, but it won't affect how the end form looks. Start with the scaled drawing on your block of foam as described in steps 1 and 2. Use your available cutting tools to remove edges, planes, and larger chunks. Use the wire brush tool aggressively to remove material, rather than just to refine the surface. A wire wheel attachment on a power drill can be a big time saver, but it only works on larger pieces of foam, or on smaller pieces that can be secured. Wear goggles and a dust mask so you don't have to experience just how uncomfortable the pesky polystyrene foam beads can be if they get in your eyes and nose.

This is another instance where you want to stop periodically to assess the progress of your work. As you're working, re-establish your lines by drawing with the marker on your foam. If you're carving a symmetrical piece, continually check your measurements. If you're making an armature for a seating unit, sit in it as your work develops (see the Garden Throne on page 140).

I like to carve the foam to the size and contour I have planned for the finished piece. When I'm satisfied with the shape, I consider how the piece will be finished. If I plan to first apply concrete and then cover the surface with mosaic, I know that I'll be adding approximately 1 inch (2.5 cm) to the finished surface. Returning to the polystyrene foam armature, I'll continue carving to remove that 1 inch (2.5 cm) over the whole surface so the piece won't be too bulky when finished.

A polystyrene foam core is versatile and easily adapted or modified. If you need to add metal supports for a sculpture to make it more structurally sound, or if you need to incorporate attachments or connecting systems, the foam can be cut in half, and a form-fitting channel can be hollowed out, using small wire brushes or rifflers to secure the required additions.

ADAPTING A POLYSTYRENE FOAM CORE FOR A TOTEM CONSTRUCTION

A totem construction is an exciting way to create a larger, more complex piece of sculpture. Essentially, you're creating a series of smaller pieces that get stacked together to make a larger statement. Once you have your basic idea, or ideas, use the preceding instructions to carve a series of polystyrene foam shapes. (See the information on "The Ensworth Project," page 81.)

Additional Materials and Tools

— PVC pipe
— Straightedge
— Small wire brush or riffler rasp
— Construction caulk adhesive
— Large construction nails

Instructions

1
Once you've finished carving the core, draw a center line to guide you as you cut the piece in half.

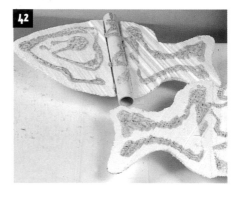

2
With the cut halves facing up, decide how you'd like to position the piece on the pole, taking into consideration the weight of the finished piece and how it will physically balance on your totem.

3
Measure and mark the outside width of your PVC pipe onto the polystyrene foam.

4
Measure the length of the area where the pipe will be inserted, and add 2 inches (5.1 cm) to the length. Cut a piece of pipe to that length.

5
Use the riffler rasp to carve out a hollow space, half the circumference of the pipe on one side (photo 40).

6
Hold the two halves of the polystyrene foam together. Use the permanent marker to mark the opening of the first carved half, transferring the measurements onto the opposite side. Lay the sections down and connect the marks using the straightedge.

7
Carve out the second half as in step 5.

8
When you put the two pieces together with the pipe inserted, the pieces should fit together tightly and the pipe should be snug.

9
Glue all the pieces together using the caulk adhesive by first applying a generous bead of the adhesive onto both sides of the pipe and the foam.

10
Put the pieces together (photo 41) and then immediately pull them apart (photo 42). Allow the adhesive to air dry for approximately 10 minutes, and then reposition the sections. This contact method provides a stronger initial bond and will make it easier to work with the piece sooner.

11
Secure the edges with a few long nails for added strength. For larger pieces, I've even used landscaping nails to pin sections together.

Carving Basics

When sculpting, you either add or subtract material to create a form. Carving is about subtracting. A rough translation of a response from Michelangelo when asked how he could carve a figure from stone is, "The figure was in the stone. I just removed everything that wasn't the figure." In other words, you need to be able to visualize the form you want to carve before you begin.

If you were carving stone, you'd select one with the approximate proportion of the form you wanted to carve. One of the benefits of carving in concrete is that you can easily cast a block or shape with the proportions you need. To decide on the size and proportion of your casting, you might want to work on a preliminary design for your carving. This will help you solve problems on a small scale, saving you time and materials. You don't want to cast a very large block of concrete for a relatively small piece and spend all your energy removing excess material.

If you want to start with a sketch, try to draw the image from different views as if you were looking at it from the front, the sides, and even from above, or what is sometimes called a bird's-eye or overhead view. Draw these views to scale to work out the finished proportions. Sculpture is a three-dimensional art form, so you might prefer to develop your ideas dimensionally; working with clay to

Elder G. Jones, *Wall*, 1996, 20 to 30 inches (50.8 to 76.2 cm) high. Carved concrete. Photo by artist

create a small model or maquette can be useful. It is beneficial to see and feel the different views of a piece.

While your carving methods may be adjusted according to the scale of your work, you should always position your carving at a level that is comfortable to work on so that your back and arms are in a natural position. Also, place your work on a sturdy surface that can maintain the weight of the piece as well as the impact of any carving.

If the piece is too large to move easily, try to locate it so you can walk and work around the piece. Or, place the piece on a turntable or lazy Susan so you can turn it. Sometimes small pieces need to be tilted to accomplish certain cuts. Use sandbags to prop and reposition a piece; they'll also help absorb the shock of the carving blows. A fast and easy method of creating sandbags is to take some old jeans or other sturdy-fabric trousers and cut off the legs. Sew up one end of the leg, fill it two-thirds full of sand, and sew up the open end.

Often, when people start to carve, they're timid about taking off too much material. Don't be! You want to transform your cast form, and concrete needs to be removed, sometimes in large chunks. If you're carving a head from a block that you have cast, you want to lose the squareness of the initial casting. Start by making wide cuts until you see the basic form begin to emerge. Don't get too involved with one small area or detail. Continue to work on the piece in a holistic way, constantly turning it or moving

Jack Hastings, *Masked Beast*, 1976, 24 x 24 x 15 inches (61 x 61 x 38.1 cm). Wet-carved concrete.
Photo by Elder Jones

WET CARVING

The advantage of carving concrete just after it has set is that the material can be removed quickly. There's also very little dust as you work on your piece. The following technique uses a stepping stone as an example, but these same steps can be adapted to create larger forms, such as the Rousseau Relief Planter on page 121 and the Figurative Table Base on page 134. The tools used for this technique don't have to be fancy. You can easily collect a variety of toothed tools by picking up a package of assorted blades for a reciprocating saw at your local hardware store. Or just modify some old saw blades that are lying around your shop. A visit to the kitchen area of a local thrift shop will probably provide you with a variety of knives and utensils that can be adapted.

Materials and Tools

CONCRETE MIX: Premixed Sand (Topping) Mix, Sifted, or Mix 4
— Materials to construct your casting form
— Plastic work board
— Container to mix concrete
— Trowel
— Turntable or lazy Susan
— Awl, large nails, or other sharp-pointed tools
— Assorted sharp knives
— Assorted toothed and flat tools
— Whisk broom

This form was made with strips of aluminum flashing held together with small clamps and reinforced by tying a cord around the flashing.

around it to develop your form. Work with your tools so that you're carving away from high points or protrusions, such as a nose on a face. You don't want to accidentally lop off a nose! If there's no other direction to work, establish a stop line by making a cut or slice in the concrete in front of the protrusion, and carve only to the depth of that line.

Concrete can be carved by different methods at the different set stages. The results, tools used, and energy expended will vary at each stage. You might start carving a piece with the wet technique and finish it using the dry technique. This is how I approached the Ancient Carving on page 115.

Wet carving tools. Clockwise from top left: float, masonry trowel, pointing trowel, kitchen knives, shaped metal scrapers, more kitchen knives, assorted modified saw blades

Instructions

1

Select or build your form, and position the work board (photo 43). This will be the board that you'll be executing your carving on later. Working on a piece of plastic or a board with a plastic laminate surface will provide a surface that is both non-stick and sturdy.

2

Mix the concrete to a creamy texture, about the consistency of muffin batter.

3

Fill your mold by starting in the middle to avoid creating air pockets as the form is filled. Agitate or wiggle the board to eliminate air bubbles.

4

Use the trowel to level off the concrete in your form (photo 44).

5

Allow the concrete to set until it's firm, but not hard. If the temperature is 70° to 75°F (21° to 24°C), this will probably take about three hours.

6

Move the casting to a sturdy table to carve. Place the work board and the mold on the turntable or lazy Susan to make it easier to work around the carving.

7

Remove the form (photo 45).

8

Use a saw blade tool to scrape off the top scale, or the flaky, crystaline deposit caused by the evaporated water. This gives the surface a consistent, grainy texture (photo 46).

9

Draw out the design with a sharp knife or pointed tool (photo 47).

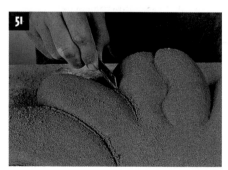

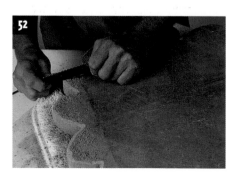

10

Block or rough out the shape by cutting it out with the sharp knife (photo 48).

11

Use a coarse saw blade or other toothed tool to shave and scrape as you begin to refine the shape (photo 49). As you're scraping or shaving the concrete off the form, work each stroke at a right angle to the previous stroke. You want to constantly change the direction of your carving stroke as you work across the piece to achieve a consistent surface texture.

12

Use a flat-edged tool to smooth the surface while you work each stroke at right angles to one another (photo 50). Don't touch the surface with your fingers. Overworking your piece or directly handling it will change the surface texture.

13

Redefine the edges and lines using the sharp point of a knife (photo 51).

14

Softly brush the surface with a whisk broom to unify the surface texture. The brushing functions almost like a light sanding.

15

After you're finished carving, leave the piece uncovered overnight.

16

The next day, carefully turn the piece over onto a soft surface, such as a piece of carpet, so that the surface won't get scratched.

Carved stepping stones make an eclectic garden path.

17

Using a flat piece of metal, remove the sharp bottom edge by scraping at an angle (photo 52).

18

While the piece is upside down, you might also sign and date your piece with a sharp nail.

19

Take the piece outside and spray it with water to remove the remaining dust. Don't be dismayed if there are small round holes on the surface. These are just air bubbles and are part of the process.

20

To cure, wrap in a wet towel, then in plastic, and leave for five days.

DRY CARVING

Concrete is often referred to as cast stone. You can approach cured concrete like stone. In fact, you'll use many of the same tools and safety precautions. Wear a good dust mask and goggles.

The selected aggregate will have a significant effect on how the material reacts to the carving tools. Fine aggregates, such sand or powdered marble, are going to produce a material that has a texture like limestone. If you use vermiculite or perlite, the material will be much softer, and you'll even be able to saw it, depending on the ratio of those aggregates. A hard-crushed stone aggregate will make a material that's much harder and less effective to carve.

Materials and Tools

Assorted chisels: If you're carving cast material using a soft aggregate, such as vermiculite or perlite, you'll be able to use wood chisels. If you have cast a block with sand or marble dust, carbide-tipped stone chisels are recommended.

Assorted files, rasps, and rifflers: In addition to flats and bastards, curved face files, rifflers, small curved files and rasps used by sculptors will help to refine surfaces and develop detail.

Wire brush: Whenever you're using a file or rasp, you should always have a wire brush close at hand to remove the grit from the tools' teeth and to clean the files when you're finished using them.

4½-inch (11.4 cm) power grinder with masonry or diamond-surfaced wheel attachments: This can be an effective tool throughout the carving process. It can be used as a cutting tool to rough out the shape in the beginning; as a carving tool while you remove material to further define your forms; and as a finishing tool that can either smooth the surfaces of your carving or add interesting textures and lines.

Direct Modeling

Most people think of concrete as a poured material. In fact it's capable of being shaped or formed in a number of ways. By controlling the

Pedro Silva, *Sea Monster*, 1981, detail of Dragon Park. Concrete hand formed over a steel and mesh armature; mosaic surface treatment. Photo by Sherri Warner Hunter

amount of water added to your materials, several of the recipes on pages 28 and 29 will produce a concrete with a consistency similar to clay, which can be modeled very effectively. Modeling with concrete works best as a *relief*, a low level form emerging from a flat surface, or built up over an armature. Consistency is one consideration when modeling; gravity is another. If you're modeling a face, you can't fully shape the nose in wet concrete and expect it to remain in place. It will begin to droop and slide. A modeled concrete form should be built up in layers, allowing each to set before adding more. If you're patient with the material, the end results will be gratifying.

You can create a whole piece with the modeling technique, or use it to give interesting contrast to a piece that employs other surface decorations, such as the faces that punctuate the mosaic arches of the sea monster in the photo on page 55, created in Nashville, Tennessee, by a community collaboration with artist Pedro Silvas.

MODELING A HUMAN FACE

When working on a modeled piece, either mix several small batches of concrete at a time, using a small plastic container to measure your parts, or, if you've been working on other pieces, use the remaining concrete after it has begun to set for an hour or two. I usually have more success with the latter. I often try to move too quickly with freshly mixed concrete, and spend more time than necessary trying to keep things from sliding.

Materials and Tools

CONCRETE MIX: Premixed Sand (Topping) Mix or Mix 3 or 10; Slurry Mix 14 or 16
— Base form or armature materials
— Latex surgical gloves
— Container to mix concrete
— Container to mix slurry
— Paintbrush
— Sponge
— Short pieces of ¼-inch (6 mm) dowels, sharpened in a pencil sharpener
— Assorted artist brushes (I use brushes that have been worn out from painting rather than new ones. My favorites are a ¼-inch [6 mm] short, flat sable, and a soft, round #10 watercolor brush.)
— Assorted wooden or wire-end clay or sculpture tools (optional)
— Plastic drop cloths
— Kitchen knife
— Rasps or riffler rasps (optional)
— File (optional)

Instructions

1
Select a preconstructed base surface, or build the armature to model on to. First, add one or two applications of concrete to fill out the armature or create your modeling surface.

2
Each time you return to a piece that's in progress, remove or file any unwanted concrete areas, and spray the piece with water.

3
Lightly slurry the surface you'll be adding concrete to, and allow it to dry just long enough for it to lose the surface shine.

4
When you begin to model your form, consider where the highest points of the form will be located. For a face, you'll want to begin to define the forehead, cheekbones, nose, and chin. Start to build these sections by adding small pinches of concrete, taking time to compress each application as you go so no air pockets are created (photo 53). Use a damp sponge to push and compress the material as

you're working. If you're working on a vertical surface, always try to exert pressure in an upward motion.

Note: In the beginning stages of forming, the piece will look awkward and clumsy. (See photos!) Don't get critical or discouraged. Enjoy the process. You'll have lots of opportunities to make changes to the piece.

5

Don't get involved with details at this point. Add the material without focusing on any one area. Establish the location or proportion of the features (photo 54). If you notice any sliding or distortion, restrain yourself from continuing. Cover the piece with plastic, and allow it to setup for at least 30 minutes before proceeding.

6

File or remove any unwanted concrete, and mist the piece with water, if the surface appears dry.

7

Proceed again with small applications of concrete to better establish the features (photo 55). Use the sharpened dowel to help define lines or creases, such as the eyelids. Soften the lines by dipping the artist's brushes in water, squeezing out the excess moisture, and brushing over the sharp lines. Think of the dowel, brushes, or any other tools you might use, as extensions of your own hands. They can help to define areas by pushing and moving small amounts of concrete that would be difficult to manipulate with your fingers (photo 56).

Note: Whether you're modeling or carving, definition in a sculpted form occurs in the way light and shadow play on the surface of a form. Stylistically, there will be times when you want to create a very smooth form; however, looking at the eyes in photo 56, notice how the shadow cast by the narrow ridge of the upper lids adds to the appearance of depth in the eyes. Consider how edges and shadows will add depth and the illusion of volume to your piece.

8

Refine areas with a damp sponge or a paintbrush dipped in water.

9

If you plan to combine a modeled element with other surface treatments, consider how much more concrete you'll need to add to incise or texture an area, or how deep a space you'll need to leave to accommodate mosaic or embedding.

10

Repeat steps 2 and 7 until you're satisfied with your form.

Concrete Systems

Technical advances in the engineering of concrete and in concrete additives are occurring every day. Adding polymer fortifiers, polyester or polypropylene fibers, or alkali-resistant fiberglass to cement, results in a material that is superior in strength and durability. New systems being used in the building industry utilize a combination of these materials to create stucco-like finishes on new industrial construction. Some variations of these materials are readily available at home improvement centers, while others, due to their unique qualities, need to be ordered from specialized suppliers.

POLYADAM CONCRETE SYSTEM

As I explored techniques to construct large-scale concrete sculptures, I was introduced to this system by my former sculpture instructor, Dale Eldred. He used this system for a commission to design stage sets for the Kansas City Ballet's production of *An American in Paris*. The set elements had to be lightweight enough to be raised and lowered during the performance, but durable enough to travel with the company to different venues. This particular system, developed by George E. Adamy, combines a high-quality acrylic polymer additive, Polyadam II or PII, portland cement, sand, and *glass scrim*, an alkali-resistant, fiberglass reinforcing material that's compatible with cementitious products. The resulting structures are strong, light-weight, and weather resistant, and, unlike a resin-based fiberglass system, the materials are nontoxic.

Another attractive quality of this system is that it can be applied to virtually any surface. Its strength is derived from its unique combination of materials. An otherwise structurally weak armature only needs to function until the system sets. After that, the cured strength of the shell supersedes the strength of the interior supporting structure. This enables you to start with armature or base forms created from materials such as foam rubber, cardboard, or even stuffed fabric.

As my own work has developed, I've come to prefer using this system to cover carved polystyrene foam armatures. The Garden Throne on page 140 and Bird Watching on page 137 are two examples. The methods I utilize for shaping the polystyrene foam are detailed under Chapter 2: Polystyrene Foam Armatures on pages 47 through 49.

When I mix these materials, I use a small measuring container. Due to the cost of the supplies, I'd rather mix another small batch to complete a piece than throw expensive materials away.

POLYADAM CONCRETE SYSTEM APPLIED OVER A POLYSTYRENE FOAM FORM

With this system you can make a strong and surprisingly lightweight form that's waterproof.

Materials and Tools
CONCRETE MIX: Mix 9 and 10; Slurry Mix 16
— Polystyrene foam form
— Polyadam II
— Lightweight glass scrim
— Heavy-duty glass scrim
— Scissors
— Permanent marker
— Container to mix concrete
— Container to mix slurry
— Paintbrush
— 4 mil plastic
— Galvanized roofing nails
— Lightweight wire
— 2 mil plastic
— Rasp or rub block
— Hammer (optional)

Instructions

1
Use the scissors to cut the light-weight glass scrim into strips. The amount and size of your strips depends on the shape of the armature form you want to cover. The

The Polyadam Concrete System allows you to create incredibly durable, yet light-weight structures.

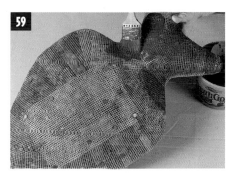

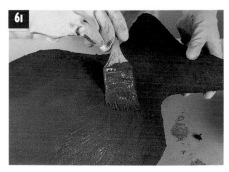

more small curves there are, the thinner you should make the strips. Large, flat areas can be covered by wide strips. I usually cut stacks of 2, 3, and 6-inch-wide (5.1, 7.6, and 15.2 cm) strips approximately 18 inches (45.7 cm) long. Any of these can be cut shorter as you're working. Cutting the 6-inch (15.2 cm) strips into squares can be very useful as well. Set aside until needed.

2

To prepare your heavy scrim, you'll need to cut large sections to completely cover your shape. There are two ways to approach this. The first way would be to tack a length of mesh onto the carved shape using the roofing nails. Trace the shape using a permanent marker. When you cut out the mesh, add an additional ½ inch (1.3 cm) all the way around the tracing. An alternative method would be to tack paper over the form, and make a paper pattern that can then be traced onto the heavy mesh. Don't forget to add the ½ inch (1.3 cm) to your pattern. This will allow you to save material by arranging your pattern as conservatively as possible onto the mesh. Set the sections aside until needed.

3

Place your form on a plastic-covered work area.

4

Mix the slurry, and slurry the entire piece (photo 57).

5

Apply the lightweight mesh, overlapping each strip by ¾ inch (1.9 cm) or more, much in the way you would

apply papier-mâché (photo 58). Secure each piece tightly to the foam surface with the roofing nails. Continue until the entire form has been covered. Use as many nails as needed to ensure a secure application of mesh. Don't worry if some areas appear to have more overlapped material than others. In fact, you may want to use additional mesh to reinforce weaker areas of your form, like the tail of this fish.

6

Mix the concrete. Apply another coat of slurry over the mesh (photo 59), and then apply your concrete. Take small handfuls and rub it over the surface as if you're pushing soft cheese through a cheese grater (photo 60). Make sure that the concrete is worked between the layers of mesh and is compressed against the foam. Cover the entire form with concrete.

7

Use the slurry paintbrush to level the concrete by brushing lightly over the surface (photo 61).

8

Cover with 2 mil plastic, and leave undisturbed overnight.

9

The next day, use the rasp or block over the whole surface to remove any rough areas.

10

Mix another batch of slurry, and apply it to the form.

11

Attach the heavy mesh sections to your form with roofing nails. It may be necessary to cut slits or darts into

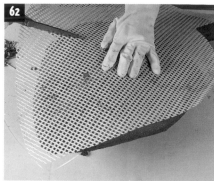

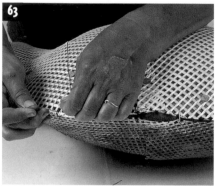

the mesh so that the mesh will conform to the contour of the form (photo 62). Secure the mesh with as many nails as needed to ensure that it lies firmly against the surface. You may need to use a hammer to tap the nails through the first layer.

12
Wire together edges where sides meet to secure the mesh sections (photo 63).

13
Slurry the mesh (photo 64), and then cover the form with concrete, using the same grating method described in step 6 (photo 65).

14
Even the surface as described in step 7. Cover with plastic, and leave undisturbed overnight.

15
The next day, use the rasp or block over the whole surface to remove any rough areas.

16
A third application of concrete will help to refine the form, give the surface a finished texture, or allow you to build up additional detail.

Note: When I make small shapes as decorative, rather than structural elements, such as a bird for a totem, I'll usually only apply the lightweight mesh, overlap the material more extensively, and apply a second coat of the concrete to refine the form. To order PII and glass scrim, see page 143.

George E. Adamy, *Notched Ring*, 1980, 13 x 3 x ⁵/₈ inches (33 x 7.6 x 1.6 cm). Portland cement, sand, Polyadam II, glass scrim; PCS casting in plastic mold with polystyrene armature embedded; untreated, uncolored surface. Photo by artist

Surface Treatments

Sometimes a natural concrete surface is all you need or want. Other times, you may want to add color or texture, or use a concrete form as a surface to mosaic. The options for surface treatments or finishes are as varied as the forms you can create with concrete.

Certain finishes can only be applied to dry, cured concrete to avoid blistering or efflorescence. Other surfaces are achieved with additives or the manipulation of the final application of concrete to your form. Explore these techniques, and maybe through experimentation you'll come up with some finishes of your own.

Surface Textures

The spontaneous movement of the concrete, as it has been applied by hand or trowel, speaks of how the piece was created, while a brushed or sponged surface might indicate how a material that was once liquid was smoothed into control. You can manipulate the surface texture of concrete at each stage of the set process from the initial application to the cured hard surface. The consistency of the material will dictate the type of marks or finishes that can be applied.

Further exploration of the masonry techniques of the construction trade can add to your mark-making vocabulary. Professionals who pour patios and walkways have all sorts of tools, methods, and materials to create a wide range of finish textures. Others who work with stucco or plaster finishing can provide insights to the application of wet materials to create decorative patterns.

Virginia Bullman and LaNelle Davis, *Time Passage*, 1999, 7 x 5 x 2 feet (2.1 x 1.5 x .6 m). Peace Garden, Funky Chicken Art Project, Dahlonega, GA. Cement formed over chicken wire armature. Photo by Hank Margeson

INCISING ON THE SURFACE OF A BASE FORM

If, in your youth, you ever took a stick and wrote your name into a freshly poured concrete sidewalk, then you already have experience with this technique. Incising is the process of cutting, carving, or drawing into the surface of semi-set concrete with a sharp instrument. You can incise designs, words, or your signature into your concrete creations. Use this technique as a surface treatment to finish a base form or to decorate the surface of a casting.

Materials and Tools

CONCRETE MIX: Premixed Sand (Topping) Mix, Mortar Mix, or Mix 3; Slurry Mix 14

— Container to mix concrete

— Container to mix slurry

— Paintbrush

— Incising tool: your tool can be a pencil (I find a dull one works better than a freshly sharpened one), a short piece of ¼-inch (6 mm) wood dowel that's been sharpened in a sharpener, a nail, or an awl—whatever feels comfortable in your hand. Experiment with other mark-making tools. A bent piece of pipe can make a clean deep groove, while a broken piece of comb can make a rough, scratchy surface.

— Artist's paintbrush

Instructions

1
Spray the base form with water.

2
Mix your slurry and cement.

3
Brush the slurry onto the base form, and apply a coat of concrete at least ¼ inch thick (6 mm).

4
Work the surface of your piece until you're satisfied with the overall texture.

5
Allow the concrete to become slightly stiff, and wait for most of the water to evaporate from the surface.

6
Select the tool(s) you want to use to make your incised design.

7
Sketch the design or words very lightly in the surface. If you need to make some changes in how the design is positioned, refinish and try again.

8
Once you're satisfied with the sketched design, use your tool so that it's at about a 45° angle to the concrete surface. You're not just writing or drawing, but pushing the tool into the concrete. Don't push too deeply on the first pass.

9
If your lines fill with water, let the surface moisture evaporate longer before proceeding.

10
Retrace your lines, pressing slightly deeper so that the finished depth of the line is approximately ¼ inch (6 mm) or a level that looks good to you. Remove any accumulated concrete on your tool with each stroke.

11
Allow the concrete to continue to set until all surface moisture is gone. Use the artist's paintbrush to soften the

Marvin and Lilli Ann Killen Rosenberg, *Walkway with Planter (detail)*, 2000, Stephen's Place Affordable Housing Project, Medford, OR. Colored concrete fish; slate, mosaics, inlaid shells, stones, and bones; incising. Photo by Marvin Rosenberg

the artist's paintbrush to soften the lines. Dip the brush in water, squeeze out the excess moisture, and brush lightly over the lines. Rinse and repeat as needed.

12
Follow the same instructions for incising the surface of a casting. Screed and/or trowel the top surface to your desired smoothness and then incise.

STAMPING

Use old printing blocks, rubber stamps, cookie cutters, various sizes of tin cans, and even buttons, shells, and plastic toys to press into the surface of semi-set concrete. Check the kitchen for implements, such as cookie presses or potato mashers, to use to add interesting textural elements. Simply dip the "stamp" in water, shake off the excess moisture, position on the surface, and press to your desired depth.

In case you're thinking about stamping a much larger area, say a patio, commercial stamping tools are available at most large rental centers that can imprint simulated paving brick, stone, tile, or other patterns.

TEXTURES IN FRESH CONCRETE

As you apply concrete to a form either by hand or with a tool, you'll notice a unique impression or mark that's the result of that application. As the application continues and the mark is repeated, a texture begins to emerge. Trowels, palette knives,

table knives, and small putty knives are all going to produce different textures, depending on how you stroke or apply the wet concrete. Distinctive marks made by hand applications of pinches of concrete or dents in a modeled surface will add to the personality of your work. Each tool and each person leaves its own unique set of marks, so the possibilities of new and interesting textures are virtually limitless.

TOOL MARKS IN HARDENING CONCRETE

As we've seen in Carving Basics in Chapter 2, set concrete can be cut with a knife, and an emerging form can be developed with small sections of saw blades. A coarse rasp cut across a surface creates a series of small lines that serve not only to form your piece but to add surface texture as well. There is another type of rasp has sharp holes like a cheese grater that can slice through soft concrete, leaving flatter, but still distinctive, lines.

As concrete continues to harden into a rock-like mass, stone-carving tools, such as a flat or toothed chisels and points, can be used to create still other textures. This effect can be heightened in a piece by contrasting different surface textures to accentuate the forms of your design; incorporate smooth restful areas to set off busy textured ones.

Polished Concrete

Artist Lynn Olson has inspired thousands of sculptors to see concrete in a completely different way. Not only has he generously shared his knowledge of construction techniques to expand our thinking of how concrete can be utilized as a direct application material, but his polished sculptures have literally transformed how we look at concrete surfaces.

When asked how he accomplishes such beautiful concrete surfaces, Lynn has two answers.

The short answer: elbow grease!

The long answer: As portland cement combines with water, it forms tiny crystals of calcium silicate hydrate that are too small to see. Like finely grained stones, these crystals can be cut and polished to create a smooth surface. The process is similar to that of finishing any stone, with one main exception: the mixture created with portland cement hardens slowly over days, weeks, and even months. The polishing process can actually begin before the mixture is hard—a significant advantage over trying to polish natural stone.

Most people don't expect to see smooth and polished cement because they usually see cement used in combination with sand and gravel in concrete. The visible sand in the concrete is, of course, always rough and dull. However, replace the typical aggregates with marble or other silica-based dusts and metallic fibers, and you have a sensitive material, rich in aesthetic potentials.

You may decide to only polish a portion of your sculpture rather than the whole piece. This will enable surface textures to contrast one another and add interest to your piece.

POLISHING A SCULPTURE

As you proceed through the steps of polishing, notice the marks that the various tools you're using leave on the cement surface. There may be a point in time that you choose to utilize that texture as a finished surface.

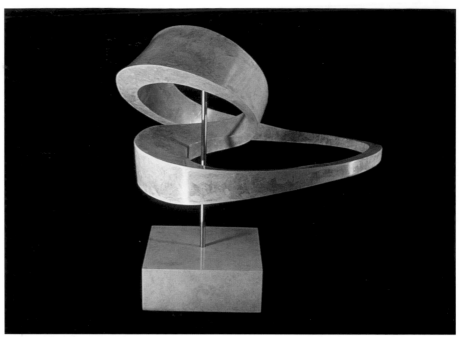

Lynn Olson, *Carousel*, 1998, 24 x 24 x 19 inches (61 x 61 x 48.3 cm). Cement, stell, bronze fibers; direct modeled; polished and sealed with methyl methacrylate, blue color from reaction of bronze fibers with cement. Photo by artist

Materials and Tools

CONCRETE MIX: Mix 11 or 12; Slurry Mix 15
— Armature
— Container to mix slurry
— Paintbrush
— Container to mix concrete
— Metallic fibers
— Colored pigments (optional)
— Sharp kitchen knife
— Assorted rasps in various degrees of coarseness
— Assorted files
— Riffler rasps and files
— Wire brush to clean rasps and files
— Silicon carbide paper in various grits: grades of sandpaper may be labeled coarse, medium, or fine, or they may have a numerical code. The smaller the number, the coarser the grade of abrasive material; 40 is very coarse and 600 is very, very fine.

— Diamond abrasive tools (optional)
— Methyl methacrylate (optional)
— Wax (optional)

Instructions

1
An interesting surface can be achieved by polishing concrete mix 12. It can be applied to both fiber-cement mix 11 or sanded cement mix 3 that has been applied over an armature to create a base form.

2
Mix the slurry.

3
Mix the fiber-cement. Pigments, either iron oxides or those used in artists' paint, can be added to this final mix. First mix the fiber-cement thoroughly, and then fold in the pigments so they appear as lines of color. Don't mix in completely.

4
Brush the slurry onto the base form, and apply a thin layer, about 1/4 to 1/2 inch thick (6 mm to 1.3 cm).

5
As soon as this final application of fiber-cement sets firmly, usually in six hours or overnight, you can begin to use a variety of cutting tools to refine your form. Use a coarse rasp to cut across the surface to remove irregularities, or slice through the material with a sharp kitchen knife to define details. Work on the general surface at this stage. The material is still too soft for fine details or final finishes.

6
Allow the cement to harden further, perhaps another 24 hours. At this stage, use the coarse files and the coarsest silicon carbide abrasive paper to refine the surface, using finer and finer grades as you continue polishing.

Note: After the initial 24 hours, keep the cement surface wet while you're working on it to avoid dust and to facilitate hydration.

7

As the cement continues to harden with passing hours and days, continue to use finer files and finer grades of silicon carbide abrasive paper to develop a smoother finish.

8

Use the 600-grade silicon carbide paper to produce the final polished surface after the cement has hardened sufficiently, usually within four weeks.

9

The surface can also be burnished or rubbed firmly and methodically using the flat side of a steel blade or a traditional burnishing tool to create a luster.

10

A sealer applied to the finished piece will help to prevent stains as well as to add gloss to the surface. A water-based methyl methacrylate is recommended. It's important to use a sealer that will inhibit moisture from penetrating the surface while still allowing vapors to escape. The best way to apply it to a smooth surface is to rub it on by hand, wearing gloves, until it dries. Buff with a soft cloth to obtain a modest gloss and to enhance the colors and grain patterns in the surface. If you want more of a shine, a wax, such as carnauba wax, can be applied.

Coloring Concrete

There are three basic ways to color concrete. You can add pigments into the concrete mixture to integrate the color, stain it with transparent solutions, or apply opaque paints. In most cases, coloring processes applied to the surface of concrete should only occur after a piece has thoroughly cured and dried to avoid efflorescence, blistering, and peeling.

PIGMENTS

There are some limitations when adding color to concrete. As mentioned in earlier sections of this book, portland cement is caustic. Some pigments that work well in paint are attacked by the alkali in cement, resulting in a breakdown of the color over time. Also, *colorfastness*—if a color can endure the sun and other natural elements—is a consideration. You want to use pig-

Buddy Rhodes, *Tall Cocktail Table*, 2000, 30 inches (76.2 cm) in diameter, 44 inches (1.1 m) high. Concrete pressed into mold; integral colored concrete backfilled with contrasting concrete to create veining; ground, sanded, and sealed. Photo by Buddy Rhodes Studio

Craig Nutt, *Bridge Table*, 1997, 18 x 37 x 24 inches (45.7 x 94 x 61 cm). Polychrome concrete top, mahogany, wenge; cast concrete; color mixed into the concrete. Photo by John Lucas

ments that have been proven to last when mixed with concrete.

Typical concrete colors tend to be in the earthy range: rust, ochre, brown, and charcoal. Occasionally you'll see green or blue; however, the chemical compounds used to make these colors are significantly more expensive. Color pigments are available commercially in either a powdered form or mixed with water to form a paste or thick liquid.

Some pigments in artist acrylic paints, or concentrated pigments used to tint house paints, may have enough alkali resistance to serve satisfactorily. Bear in mind this is not

the use they were developed for. It's valuable to prepare test pieces and record your observations on how colorfast these coloring agents actually are over time.

Getting a deep, rich color also presents a problem. The maximum amount of pigment that should be added is ten percent of the weight of the mix. A higher percentage of pigment can weaken the mix, since more water is needed to wet the pigment particles, increasing the water/cement ratio of the mix. You're faced with the dilemma of deciding between a good color and a weaker concrete, or a stronger concrete and a pastel shade. Often a

base form is created without the pigment, and then a top coat of pigment and cement is applied. This creates a stronger structure with a deeply colored surface. If you plan to mix more than one batch of colored concrete for a project, be extremely careful in measuring out the proportions so you achieve uniform results.

Add pigments to a mix that uses white portland cement instead of gray to achieve cleaner-looking colors. Thorough mixing of the pigments directly into the fresh concrete will integrate the color throughout the concrete. To obtain variations in the color patterns, add the pigment after the cement has already been mixed. Don't mix thoroughly. Instead, fold in the pigments to obtain streaks of color. A polished treatment to your surface will reveal a rich pattern of color. A variation of this technique is to fold in two colors of pigment. There will be some areas where the two colors mix, and a third color will emerge as you finish the surface of your piece.

STAINS

One of the simplest methods of finishing concrete is to use a penetrating stain. This will alter the color without affecting the texture of the concrete. Acid-based stains have been specifically designed to work on concrete surfaces. When the stain is painted on the surface, the acid in the solution creates porosity by slightly etching the concrete, and the colored stain penetrates the pores of the surface.

You can also stain the surface of concrete using water-based or acrylic opaque stains. These stains are made to be used on exterior wood surfaces, so I'm not sure of the long-term colorfastness when used on concrete surfaces exposed to the weather. Apply these stains with a stiff brush, and wipe off immediately with a slightly damp cloth. This will leave the colored stain in the recessed surface textures of the concrete. As in any technique that utilizes a stain or wash, it may be necessary to apply several coats to achieve the depth of color you're looking for.

PAINTS

Artists' acrylic paints or masonry house paints, either water- or oil-based, can be used for a more solid or opaque surface color. Make sure that the piece has fully cured to ensure a lasting finish. A good masonry primer will help to prepare your surface by applying a good base and bonding coat for your final coloration. Paint tends to minimize the texture of concrete as it fills the surface pores.

Mosaic

The attraction of mosaic for me, and the aspect of this art form that'll be addressed in this section, is that by utilizing the proper materials and techniques, mosaic can provide a permanent, colorful surface on exterior works in concrete. Mosaic pieces are adhered individually onto a sculptural concrete form. This method is referred to as direct mosaic. Mosaic and embedding look similar, but the processes are quite different. Briefly, in embedding, pieces are put into wet cement; in mosaic, cement is put around the pieces (see page 76 for more on embedding).

In a mosaic, a base form in concrete must be cured and dried before

Sherri Warner Hunter, *Angel*, 1999, wall detail, Stepping Stone Park, Nashville, TN. Hand modeled over an armature; mosaic. Photo by artist

starting. The mosaic materials are attached to the surface of the base form with adhesive, leaving spaces, or *interstices*, between each piece as they're positioned. Once the adhesive has dried, a cement-based material, grout, is pushed into the spaces between each mosaic piece. The grout is cleaned off the mosaic surface and leveled between the pieces to create a solid, durable surface.

There are additional considerations when constructing an outdoor piece—mainly the weather. The biggest enemy is the freeze/thaw cycle. What we think of as changing seasons can mean death to a piece constructed from the wrong materials for a particular climate.

As you begin to accumulate supplies to use on your outdoor pieces, you need to look for frost-proof or frost-resistant materials, unless you live in an area where the temperature rarely, if ever, drops below freezing. If I'm at the local home improvement center, and I don't want to confuse the sales person by going into detail about my current garden creation, I simply ask if the material I'm looking to purchase would be good to use for my swimming pool. I don't have a swimming pool, but the concerns of moisture and year-round exposure to the elements are the same, and I get a quick yes or no answer instead of a puzzled look.

MOSAIC MATERIALS

Ceramic Tile: The basic bathroom tile that's most easily available is not suitable for outdoor use except in tropical climates. Because this type of tile is porous, moisture will migrate into the clay body of the tile. When the temperature drops, ice expands, cracking the tile. Ask for frost-proof or frost-resistant tiles. Stoneware and porcelain are the two types of clay most often used for exterior tiles, although some manufacturers will carry terra-cotta clay tiles that are frost-proof. When in doubt, ask.

Of these tiles, you'll also come to find that some are glazed and some are not. Glaze is a suspension of powdered glass that has been melted onto the surface of the tile during the firing process. Glazes can be either glossy and shiny or dull and matte. The amount of shine on the surface doesn't affect whether or not it can be used outdoors. There are also tiles that aren't glazed but have the color mixed into the clay itself. When you see these tiles, you can assume they're made from porcelain and will work well outside.

Glass: By nature, glass is an ideal material to use. Stained glass is also well suited for mosaic applications. You can purchase stained glass or ask stained glass studios for their

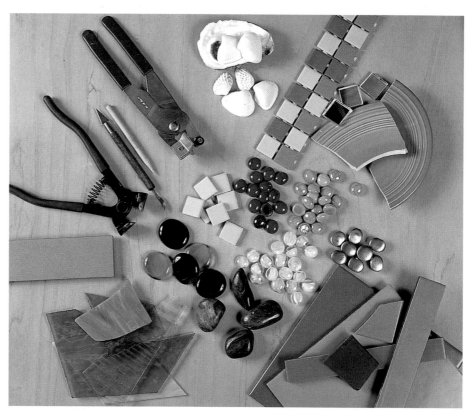

Tools and materials for mosaics. Clockwise from top center: shells, unglazed porcelain tiles, mirror, broken porcelain plates, assorted glass gems, pieces and fragments of frost-resistant glazed tile, assorted polished stones, stained glass, diamond sharpening stone, tile nippers, ceramic clean-up tool, sharpened dowel, tile cutters

scraps. Found glass, such as sea glass, broken stemware, or colored bottles, can also be used to create interesting surfaces and designs.

Mirror: The caustic chemicals in cement-based products may, over time, alter or damage mirrored surfaces, causing dull gray spots to appear; however, I use mirror because I like the initial effect, and I appreciate how nature continues to change things. Always start with a high-grade commercial mirror that is about 1/4 inch thick (6 mm), rather than a thin, low-grade material.

Broken dishes: In selecting dishes to use in your outdoor piece, follow the same advice as with ceramic tile: high-fired dinnerware and china work best. A popular reissued 1940s' dinnerware works well because it's made from porcelain. Grandmother's china may be porcelain, but you have to check carefully. In addition to checking the markings on the back of plates, I have a test that I use in the privacy of my studio, and I only mention it here as an aside. It certainly isn't scientific. I touch a piece of broken dinnerware to my tongue, and if it sticks, I assume that it's a porous, low-fire bodied dish and only suitable for interior use. If my tongue doesn't stick, I'm comfortable incorporating it into an exterior piece. We've all been told by our mothers not to put strange things into our mouths, so you decide.

Additional materials that can be used for outdoor projects include marbles, glass gems, rocks or stones, nonferrous metal objects, such as brass keys, copper pieces, silver jewelry, or other objects made from metals that don't rust. In some cases, the chemicals may cause the metals to tarnish or change colors, creating a new patina on the surface. Wood and plastic can also be used with the understanding that they're not as durable.

Mosaic Tools

Materials can be smashed with a hammer to make random pieces, or cut with a specialized saw to make precise geometric pieces. Your sense of style and design come into play as you prepare your materials to mosaic.

Safety goggles and gloves: Don't forget to protect yourself when manipulating your materials.

Hammers: Ceramic tiles and plates can be broken with a hammer safely by placing them between sections of newspaper with the glaze side down.

Tile nippers: Nippers can be used to modify larger pieces of tile or plates. They're found in the tile section of home improvement centers. You'll have more success cutting the tile if you put less of the tile in the nipper's jaws. Hold the nippers at the back of the handles; don't choke up on them. There's a curve in the jaws; position the curve so it's facing

toward the center of your body (photo 1). Hold only about 1/8 to 1/4 inch (3 to 6 mm) of the tile in the jaws of the nippers. You'll also notice that the end of the nippers is flat. Adjust the flat area so that it's pointing in the direction you'd like the tile to break. For additional leverage, hold the grip against your thigh. Squeeze the handles firmly, using one or both hands as needed. Voila! Tile nippers can also be used as a shaping tool to nibble away small sections of the plate or tile to define a shape.

Tile cutters: This tool combines two tools that are often used with stained glass. It has a carbide wheel for cutting and a pair of flange-like wings at the end that are similar to running pliers. The key thing to remember with this tool is that it's for cutting, not trimming. When you're cutting a piece in two, each section must be at least as wide as the flanges to be successful. Hold the tool handle closed, and rest the wheel on one side of the tile. Press down firmly as you move the wheel across the tile surface to the other side to score or cut a line into the surface. I do this by holding the handles at the back

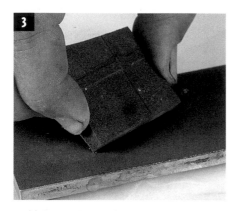

with one hand and placing the other hand on top of the tool. You want to create the score line in one pass. Don't roll the wheel back and forth or try to score the line repeatedly. If you do this correctly, the sound it'll make as you score the tile is similar to scraping your fingernails across a blackboard. Once the line is scored, open up the jaws of the tool and position them so that the spine of the tool and the

flanges are centered over the score line. Squeeze the grip slowly and firmly. The piece should break along the score line. Don't get discouraged—this tool takes practice, but once you learn to use it, you'll love it.

Tile saws: This tool can be rented from your home improvement center, or you might decide you want to invest in one if you expect to cut a lot of tile. It isn't necessary to have one to get started with mosaic.

Diamond sanding block: In some cases, when you break tile, you'll end up with a sharp edge, and when you cut tile with a saw, the edge may be slightly chipped (photo 2). I use a fine-diamond sharpening block that is actually used to sharpen knives to smooth any edges. Apply a little water to the surface of the sharpening stone, and hold the piece of tile so that the edge you want to smooth is at a 45° angle to the surface (photo 3). Then press the tile firmly against the stone, and move the piece in a circular motion four to six times, or until the chips are removed and the edge is smooth (photo 4).

ADHERING THE MOSAIC TO YOUR BASIC FORM

The selection of adhesive for any project depends on the surfaces you're trying to adhere and where and how the piece is going to be used. For concrete base forms that are covered in ceramic and glass mosaic, I recommend a polymer-fortified thin-set adhesive. This is the

same thin-set used for most tile floor and swimming pool installations. It's available in gray or white because it's a portland-based product. If you have a choice, select the white. If you're using gems or stained glass, the white adhesive will provide a uniform background visible through the transparent mosaic material, and the colors will appear clearer and brighter.

The polymers added to thin-set are either in a powdered or liquid form. Some thin-sets have powdered polymers that are combined with the other dry ingredients during the manufacturing. All you do is add water to activate the polymers. Other companies market a two-part product that has a dry component and a milky white liquid containing the polymers, known simply as "milk." The two parts are mixed together without any additional water. It's very important to read the directions on the package of the thin-set you are considering. If a product needs to have the separate liquid polymers added to it, and you only add water, the pieces may stick initially, but may not provide a waterproof bond to make them permanent. Only mix small batches at a time. I have a collection of plastic food storage containers with snap-on lids I use as mixing containers. Put about ½ cup (112 g) of dry mix into the container, and add 1 or 2 ounces (28 or 56 g) of the milk (photo 5). Stir the two ingredients together until the mixture is the consistency of peanut

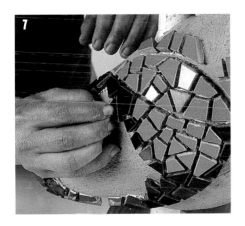

butter. Allow the mixture to sit for about five minutes, and stir again until you get a creamy consistency. When I'm not using the mixture, I snap the lid on to extend the *pot life*, or the amount of time that the mixture is workable. Occasionally I'll add a few drops of the milky liquid to the adhesive if it gets a little too stiff. Generally, if I've been careful about covering my container when not in use, I'll be able to use the mixture for three to four hours.

The technique I use to apply the adhesive to the surface is called *buttering*. I like to compare it to putting peanut butter on crackers (photo 6). I use old table knives to apply the mosaic adhesive. It's important to cover the entire surface of the mosaic piece, regardless of its size. You don't want to *starve* the joint by not applying enough adhesive. You also don't want to have so much adhesive on the back that it comes oozing around the piece as you stick it on. I like to generously cover the back surface of the mosaic material with adhesive and then lightly scrape off the excess on the side with the knife blade angled, so the remaining adhesive forms a low pyramid in the center of the piece. When the mosaic piece is applied to the base form with light pressure, the adhesive levels, and a good bond is created (photo 7). Any adhesive that oozes out is removed using the knife or a ceramic cleanup tool (photo 8). Allow the thin set to dry for at least 24 hours before grouting.

GROUTING

Grout is a cement-based material that is applied to fill the spaces between the mosaic pieces. In fact, your grout lines should be considered an important aspect of your mosaic design. The wider the spaces between your mosaic materials, the more dominant the color of the grout will be in your finished piece. You can vary the thickness of your grout lines to help define a shape or design. There are two different types of grout: unsanded and sanded. The unsanded is typically used for interior application where the spaces between tiles are uniform and 1/8 inch (3 mm) or less, and has a consistency more similar to plaster. When spaces are larger than 1/8 inch (3 mm) or are irregular, you should use sanded grout. Most sanded grouts are mixed with liquid polymers or contain polymers in the dry mix. Polymers always add flexibility to the finished material, making it suitable for exterior use.

Most home improvement centers sell a brand of fortified sanded grout in a variety of colors. You can also use the Basic Sand Mix 3, as a grout. Add your own color to customize your grout if you wish. If you're grouting a larger piece, be sure to measure your pigment additives carefully so you don't end up with a different shade for each batch. The color you choose for your grout can set off a design or wash it out. Bright or dark colors of grout tend to fade when used outside. So choose your grout color carefully.

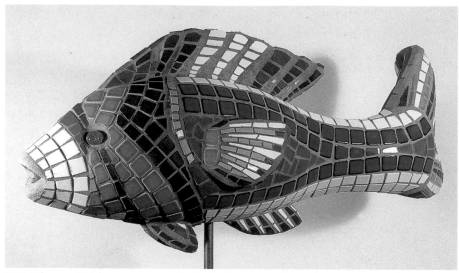

Nina Solomon, *Fish*, 1999, 14 x 9 x 34 inches (35.6 x 22.9 x 86.4 cm). Cement over polystyrene foam and mesh armature; mosaic. Photo by artist

Grouting seems to be one of life's little mysteries. It's not that difficult, although it can be labor intensive, depending on the scale of your piece and how textural the mosaic is. The grouting process needs to be worked through to completion once you begin. You can't stop in the middle of grouting to go out for dinner. It's best to get everything organized, and block out the time needed to do a good job grouting.

GROUTING A MOSAIC SURFACE

If you can physically hold the piece you want to grout, such as a bird or a planter, allot about four hours for the complete grouting process from setup to cleanup. If the piece is larger, enlist the help of assistants, and plan on a six-hour work session.

Materials and Tools

— Container to mix grout

— Grout mix

— 4 mil plastic

— Sponge

— Cheesecloth

— Spray water bottle

— Blanket (optional)

Instructions

1

Mix the grout following package directions or the custom recipe. If you have a large bag of grout, but only want to mix a small amount, the basic proportions are 4 to 1—four parts of powdered mix to one part water. When mixed properly, grout should have the consistency of sugar cookie dough—a no-slump consistency that does not crumble. Allow the mixture to sit about five minutes so that the moisture can be absorbed by the grout particles. Mix again so that it feels workable and even in texture.

2

Wearing rubber gloves, take a small handful, and using the heel of your palm, compress it onto the surface of your form using a small circular motion. Continue to rub the mixture until most of the material is off of the mosaic surface. Take your next handful, and, overlapping the initial area slightly, apply it in the same manner. Continue to do so until the entire mosaic has been filled with grout.

3

Allow the grout to set up until firm. For a smaller piece, you may need to wait 20 minutes or so. For larger pieces, it may have taken so long to apply the grout that it's already firm enough to proceed with the next step in the area where you started.

4

Level the grout between the mosaic pieces. Dip the sponge in water, squeeze it almost dry, and rub firmly, in a circular motion, over the mosaic surface to further compact the grout line and to remove deposits of grout from the mosaic. If you rub too hard in the direction of the spaces, you'll begin to remove the grout. Rubbing in a circular motion will help avoid this. Continually rinse and squeeze your sponge. Rotate the sponge as you work, always turning it to a clean side. Don't be timid about rubbing quite firmly. If you notice low spots or even holes in the grout lines, add more material, let it set up, and then sponge again as recommended. After you have leveled the grout and removed the deposits of excess material from the mosaic pieces, stop sponging.

5

Allow a haze to form over your mosaic material as the grout residue dries on the surface. The more vitreous your mosaic material is, the longer this process will take.

6

Once the haze has formed, use a clean piece of cheesecloth to buff the mosaic surface. This is the rewarding part. Throughout the process so far, the piece has looked dirty; now it begins to sparkle. To thoroughly clean the mosaic, you may need to wrap the cheesecloth over your finger and clean the surface of each individual piece. Reposition your cheesecloth as you're working so that you're always using a clean surface. Change to a clean piece of cheesecloth as needed. Three-dimensional pieces may need to be rotated in order to properly finish the complete surface. Do this with care, as the grout is still very fragile. You might want to create a soft work area by covering a folded blanket with plastic.

7

When you're finished, follow the recommended curing procedure listed on the grout package instructions. Remember, this is a cement product and it must cure properly to ensure strong grout joints. Two things that will cause cracking in grout are drying out too fast, or not compressing the material firmly into the spaces during the initial application.

REVERSE-CAST MOSAIC

The mosaic process can either be executed as a direct process or as an indirect process. The reverse-cast mosaic is an example of indirect. The stained-glass mosaic was designed by Katy Brown.

Materials and Tools

CONCRETE MIX: Premixed Sand (Topping) Mix, Mortar Mix or Mix 3

— Mold
— Paper for template
— Pencil
— Permanent marker
— Assorted frost-proof materials
— Tile nippers
— Tile cutters
— Hammer
— Newspaper
— Diamond sanding block
— Scissors
— Clear adhesive shelf paper
— 2 work boards
— Mold release agent
— Hardware cloth
— Container to mix concrete
— Screed
— 2 mil plastic
— Sponge
— Container for water
— Nylon pot scrubber

Instructions

1

On the template paper, trace the inside top surface of the mold you'll be using to cast in. Draw another line 1/4 inch (6 mm) inside that line. This space is needed to soften the edges and mold line to finish your casting. The inside area is the space you have to create your mosaic design.

2

Organize a variety of colors, shapes, and materials inside the template area, or draw a more specific design. **Note:** When you're drawing a design for mosaic, develop it in shapes rather than lines. Sketch out your design on the paper template. Use a sharp permanent marker to simplify or clarify your sketched lines. Select, break, cut, or nip your mosaic pieces, and begin to arrange the pieces for the design as if you were creating a jigsaw puzzle. Lay the pieces on top of the design template with the glaze side up. As you organize your mosaic material, make sure that you leave at least a 1/8-inch (3 mm) space between each piece. You can fill the template with consistently spaced tiles, or you can simply position a few pieces of mosaic materials. The cast concrete will create the background color.

3

When you've finished positioning your design, cut a piece of clear adhesive shelf paper to about the size of your work board.

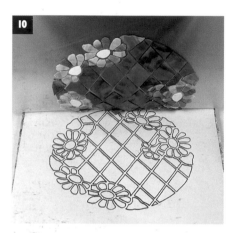

4

It helps if you have a second set of hands to help you with the next two steps, but you can do it solo if you need to. Remove the backing of the shelf paper, and hold it with the sticky side down. Hold it so it creates a "U" shape (photo 9).

5

Let the bottom curve of the shelf paper touch the center section of the mosaic design, and gently ease the sides over the rest of the design. If you try to hold the adhesive paper flat to apply it to the design, the static electricity, as well as the awkwardness of the position, will cause the design pieces to shift.

6

Rub or burnish the adhesive shelf paper over the surfaces of the mosaic materials without adhering it to the paper template.

7

After you're sure that the pieces are attached, pick up the shelf paper, which is now holding your mosaic pieces (photo 10), and turn the design upside down onto one of the work boards.

8

Apply the mold release to your mold, and center your mold over the design (photo 11).

9

With the aviator shears, cut a piece of hardware cloth ½ inch (1.3 cm) smaller than the perimeter of the mold, and set it aside.

10

Mix the concrete. Take a small handful of concrete, and press or tap it gently, but firmly, between the mosaic pieces (photo 12). You don't want the pieces to come loose from the shelf paper, and you don't want the mold to move. Continue to do this until the spaces between the mosaic materials, the interstices, are filled and the bottom surface is covered.

11

Fill the mold halfway. Position the hardware cloth so that it doesn't touch the sides of the mold, and continue filling.

12

Follow steps 9 through 13 under Casting a Simple Mold or Form (see pages 34 through 35).

13

Place a piece of plastic, then the second work board on top of the casting, so that it's now sandwiched between the two boards (photo 13). Depending on the size of the casting and your strength, you might want an assistant to help you turn it over. Hold the two pieces of wood together firmly and turn it over (as if you were taking a cake out of a baking pan).

14

Remove the shelf paper (photo 14). If there are voids in the interstices, take some of the reserved concrete and rub it into the surface in a circular motion.

15

With a damp sponge, continue to work over the surface in a circular motion (photo 15).

16

After the spaces have been filled, rinse the sponge, and start to clean the design area by continually turn-

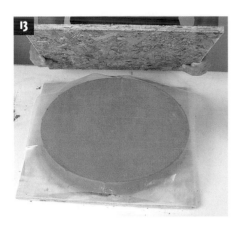

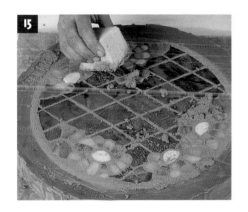

ing the sponge to clean surfaces as you wipe across the mosaic. Rinse the sponge frequently as you do this.

17

Clean off the edges of your mold (photo 16) and then remove the casting from the mold (photo 17).

18

Carefully smooth the sides, edges, and mold lines with the damp sponge (photo 18). Don't worry if there's a haze on the mosaic surface.

19

Cover with plastic and leave undisturbed overnight.

20

After 24 hours, use the soft nylon brush or nylon pot scrubber to clean the mosaic surface.

21

Keep the casting wet for five days to cure (photo 19).

I've used a stepping stone in this example, but this reverse-cast method can also be used to create decorative panels or wall hangings. Consider making a thinner mold and using extra reinforcing material to minimize the weight. You might also want to include hanging loops in the backs of these pieces when you cast them, to make installation easier.

Embedding

Embedding is the process of pushing objects into wet cement to make them part of the surface. This is a very direct process that can be spontaneous or controlled in appearance. It depends solely on the style and personality of the maker. The differences between mosaic and embedding are described in the mosaic technique section on page 67. Also refer to pages 68 through 70 for a detailed list of frost-resistant materials that are recommended for exterior embedded pieces and for a full description on how to use tools for manipulating the materials.

EMBEDDING ON A PRECONSTRUCTED BASE FORM

Embedding can be combined with several different forming techniques. It can be incorporated into the final application of concrete to base forms, such as the bowl and pedestal base of a birdbath, or utilized as the decorative surfaces in castings, such as stepping stones or sidewalks.

Materials and Tools

CONCRETE MIX: Premixed Sand (Topping) Mix, Mortar Mix or Mix 3; Slurry Mix 14

— Mosaic materials and tools (pages 68 through 70)
— Container to mix slurry
— Paintbrush
— Container to mix concrete
— Screwdriver with plastic handle
— Sponge
— Nylon brush
— Small stainless-steel brush
— Wood craft stick

Instructions

1
Prepare the base form.

2
Prepare your materials for embedding. You may want to design a recognizable image or just have a selection of materials that you'll use randomly. Often I'll decide on a few different colors of tiles and a few elements to provide added texture. I'll prepare the tiles by cutting or breaking them into certain shapes or sizes so that I have a good supply of materials on hand. I like to organize my materials in low cut cardboard boxes. Once the concrete is applied, I go to work in a method I refer to as "planned randomness." I plan on a limited palette or selection of decorative materials, and apply them in a random way. The limitation on the variety of elements helps to give the piece a sense of unity, and often, a rhythm or pattern is created subconsciously.

3
Mix the slurry and concrete.

4
Paint the slurry onto an area slightly larger than where you plan to apply the concrete (photo 20).

5
Apply an additional layer of concrete using the patty technique described on page 38 (photo 21). The layer of concrete only needs to be as thick as the thickest material you're embedding. This works easily on the inside of a bowl, which is basically a horizontal surface, but gets trickier when applied to a vertical base. When you apply this layer to a vertical surface, try not to create air pockets. Ease the cement onto the form by pushing firmly rather than trying to slap it on flat. Continually push the concrete up as it is applied to help push out any trapped air.

6
Apply as much slurry and concrete as you think you can embed within 20 minutes or so. Periodically apply more slurry and concrete so the concrete has a chance to set slightly before you begin to embed.

7
Arrange your decorative pieces on the concrete surface (photo 22).

8
When you're satisfied with the placement, use the handle of the screwdriver to firmly tap the pieces into the wet concrete (photo 23). Embed the pieces so the surface is level with the concrete.

Note: Due to displacement, you may see a small space between the embedded object and the concrete. You can either add an additional pinch of concrete, or take a wet sponge, squeeze out most of the water, and sponge over the concrete toward the center of the embedded object. This should move the concrete into that small space. If you're embedding a large, porous object, first dip it in water and then blot off the excess moisture. Adding moisture to the porous object before try-

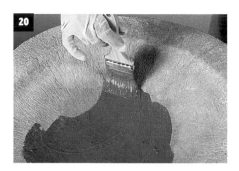

ing to embed it will keep it from absorbing too much water from the concrete. When using sea shells, fill any open spaces with concrete before embedding. This will help to reinforce the shell. If the shell gets broken and is not filled, it creates a space for water to collect, and during a freeze/thaw cycle, more damage could occur. If the shell gets broken, and it had been filled with concrete, you'll have a concrete fossil on the surface of your piece that will still look interesting.

If you find that your concrete is beginning to set up, and things are not tapping in so easily, cut out a small shape, approximately the size of the decorative element, add a dab of slurry, and then tap in the piece. Additional pinches of concrete can fill any remaining spaces.

9
Use the damp sponge to clean off large deposits of concrete and smooth the surface of the concrete (photo 24). Remember to rinse your sponge frequently and rotate it to clean surfaces as you work. Don't be concerned if a thin layer or film of concrete remains on the surface. Continued sponging is only going to smear more concrete over the surface, not clean it completely, so stop sponging.

10
When you're finished working, cover your piece loosely with plastic and leave undisturbed overnight.

11
The next day, take the piece outside and spray it with water. Use the nylon brush to clean the film off the decorative pieces. You might want to use a toothbrush-sized stainless-steel brush to clean more difficult or textural areas, but be careful that you don't scrub so hard as to scratch the concrete; it feels solid, but it hasn't yet reached its full hardness. Chunks of concrete can be pried off with the wooden craft stick. When you've finished cleaning, rinse the piece with water one last time.

If you're able to clean your piece within 12 to 24 hours of embedding, you'll find that most of the cement residue can be removed with water and elbow grease. If you're unable to work on your piece until some time later, it may be necessary to use chemicals (see page 26).

12
After you've cleaned the piece, or after the first 24 hours, cure for at least five days. If embedding a bowl, plan a work session long enough to complete the design to the edge of the bowl. If you stop work in the middle of the bowl and return to it the next day, there may be a visible line or ridge distinguishing the two applications. If you want to embellish both sides of the bowl, do one side the first day, allow that to set up for 24 hours, and do the other side on the second day.

Concrete Folk Environments
A Source of Inspiration

Looking at the work of creative people who are categorized as Folk, Naive, or Visionary Artists has provided a major source of inspiration for my work. While it's hard to come up with an encompassing label for folk artists (not, in itself, a bad thing), they're usually informally trained or self taught. I'm attracted to this type of work for several reasons: use of materials, dedication (to the project), spirit of adventure, and the sheer tenacity of the artists. There are books available that cover these artists extensively, but as a way to provide additional examples of creative concrete use and the vast possibilities that exist with concrete as the starting point, I'd like to introduce you to a few of these remarkable artists.

These are creative people on a mission, and oftentimes their work takes the form of a garden, park, or yard

Above: The Grotto of the Redemption, West Bend, Iowa (begun 1912)
Often called "The Eighth Wonder of the World," the Grotto of the Redemption was begun by Father Paul Dobberstein (1872-1954) as an homage to the Blessed Virgin Mary. By 1939, more than a million people had visited it. Father Dobberstein's work was the inspiration for many of the other grottos in the region. Work continues on the grotto.

Right: Wisconsin Concrete Park, Phillips, Wisconsin (c. 1950-1964)
Fred Smith (1886-1976) celebrated popular frontier heroes from real life, his memory, and popular folklore by creating at least 200 animal and human figures including cowboys, political figures, horse-drawn wagons, and even a large-scale Paul Bunyan.

Courtesy of the Friends of Fred Smith, Inc. and the Smith Family. Photo by Lisa Stone

Above: Ave Maria Grotto, Cullman, Alabama (c. 1932-1934)
Inspired by art history books and postcards, Brother Joseph Zoetl (1878-1961) built miniature concrete architectural replicas of Christian shrines that were placed at an abandoned quarry on the grounds of the monastery in which he lived. Many of the buildings are painted concrete, but the miniature architecture details are fashioned from items such as toilet floats and bird cages. The centerpiece of this park-like setting is a central grotto finished in 1934. Photo by Sherri Hunter

Right: Garden of Eden, Lucas, Kansas (c. 1907-1929)
The Garden of Eden is one of the oldest surviving environments in the United States. Its creator, Samuel Perry Dinsmore (1843-1931) fashioned the local limestone of Lucas, Kansas into square hewed, notched sections that resembled logs to build a three-story house. The garden contains about 50 sculptures with 30 trees all made by hand-formed concrete reinforced with steel and chicken wire armatures. One side of the half-acre property is the manifestation of his religious belief, with welcoming statues of Adam and Eve at the entry. The other side of the house is peopled by politicians and American heroes.
Photo by Sheri Fleck Rieth

show gone wacky: a unique environment. Some create out of a work ethic to be useful and to make something to give back to mankind, while others are motivated by divine inspiration, however personally translated. A man in England started his environment innocently enough: he built a concrete panda, hoping to encourage his sickly son to play out-

doors. The son was so amused that the father continued to build an amazing concrete menagerie that populated his whole garden.

Folk art environments are not specific to any one country or region. In fact they exist worldwide in countries such as India, France, England, and South Africa. They can be found

in the United States in California, Wisconsin, Georgia, and all states in between. In a few instances, a builder may have seen or heard of a predecessor's work, but for the most part, any similarity in work is more the result of a shared, collective consciousness than a direct reference.

Above: Paradise Garden, Summerville, Georgia (c. 1960-1970s)
Several concrete walls emerge from the Paradise Gardens like crazy quilts, embellished with virtually any found object imaginable, including religious statues, sections of commercially produced concrete garden sculptures, and simple castings made from discarded containers. Creator Reverand Howard Finster (b. 1924) uses his garden to illustrate his revelations and religious beliefs. Photos by Sherri Hunter

Left: Watts Towers, Los Angeles, California (c. 1924-1954)
These amazing 100-foot (30 m) towers were built from the ground up without machines, scaffolding or written plans by an Italian immigrant named Simon Rodia (1875-1965). Armatures for the towers were constructed by tightly wiring bent steel and chicken wire. As the towers grew in height, Rodia would use the structure itself as the scaffolding to climb and continue its construction using ropes to pull up supplies. Each tier or rung was embedded with discarded materials ranging from glass bottles, shells, rocks, broken tiles and plates. The whole environment is surrounded by a scallop-shaped wall. In 1954, Rodia gave the key and the title of the property to a neighbor and walked away into obscurity.
Photo by Mark Greenfield

As different as these individuals and their environments are, there are themes, building techniques, and preservation issues that link them together like distant cousins at a family reunion. Often the builders were harassed and labeled social outcasts, or at the very least, creative eccentrics. But when all was said and done, in the best case scenarios, members of the community began to see the value and uniqueness of the artist's work, and made the effort to preserve it for public enjoyment. Unfortunately, sometimes nature, time, and thoughtless individuals have won out in the destruction or damage of these amazing environments.

Community-Built Projects
Building Communities through Art

The accessibility of concrete forming and decorative techniques lends itself to the possibility of involving a wider community of people with the design, organization, and creation of an artwork. I've had the opportunity to work with broad-based community groups, and as a visiting artist in classrooms, worked with a specific community of students.

THE ENSWORTH PROJECT

The Inman Sculpture was conceived and constructed with the help of the third, sixth, and seventh graders at Ensworth School in Nashville, Tennessee. First, I worked with Heidi Welch, one of the art teachers, to identify the basic components for the

project: a totem sculpture and stepping stones. Next we estimated a budget and a time schedule for working with the students.

The third-grade students were responsible for the stepping-stone designs. To help unify the designs in the final installation, each of the three third-grade classes worked with a specific theme: water, earth, and air. The interpretation of that theme was left wide open. I was puzzled when a young man in the "air" class showed me his design of a leaf surrounded by blue. I thought he had gotten confused; then he explained that the leaf was being blown into the sky by the wind. The third graders quickly grasped the concept of arranging the

Detail of The Ensworth Project, a tribute to a special teacher. Photos by Cary Layda

A detail of the wall at Stepping Stone Park at the Salvation Army Area Command Center in Nashville, Tennessee. Photo by Gary Layda

tile piece like a jigsaw puzzle to create their designs for the reverse-cast pavers.

Before starting the totem sculpture, the older students brainstormed ideas for a theme, and then created clay models of symbols they wanted to use to represent it. The sports theme was a special tribute to Mr. Inman, a recently deceased faculty member. Students were involved in every step of the project—carving the polystyrene foam, applying concrete, and completing the mosaic surfaces. The students are proud of the piece (installed in a courtyard next to the school's gymnasium) that has become a lasting monument to their collaborative energies and to a beloved teacher.

STEPPING STONE PARK

Stepping Stone Park at the Salvation Army Area Command Center in Nashville, Tennessee, is a very special project that could only have been built with the creative energies of hundreds of volunteers. The original vision for the park was the inspiration of Reneé LaRose, a local artist who wanted to acknowledge the steps that the previously homeless residents of the Salvation Army's Transitional Housing Program were taking as they worked toward self-sufficiency. Trained as a painter, LaRose invited me to assist. The surrounding wall was formed by hand from the ground up. Rebar was bent to form 'u' shapes and then set into the ground. Cross supports and hardware cloth were wired on to complete the armature, and layers of sanded concrete mixed with

hydrated lime were troweled onto the structure in layers to form an undulating wall with sculptures emerging from the top of the wall to add interest and height.

We planned to cover the wall with brightly covered mosaic designs. Over a period of several years, hundreds of volunteers, ages 6 to 76, were asked to contribute tile designs; the only requirement was that the designs be uplifting. Mosaic designs were arranged on paper patterns, secured with transparent adhesive shelf paper, and stored until the wall was ready. Before we applied the designs to the wall, we organized various images in groupings—an underwater scene, a circus train, a sports wall—to add some continuity to the 240-foot (72 m) mosaic. The designs could be picked up and positioned because they were attached to the adhesive paper. Surrounding areas were filled in with bands of color to form stylized landscapes and the sculpture forms were also covered in mosaic.

Nine years in the making, Stepping Stone Park was funded by donations from interested individuals, organizations, and the artists themselves, and built entirely with volunteer hours. There's a special sense of pride when people come to the park and recognize their design or can point out the section of wall they helped grout. This has truly been a project for a community, built by the community.

Chapter 4

The Projects

Are you ready to mix some concrete? Before you get started, take a minute to read this. It explains how the projects are organized and offers tips that will make your projects go smoothly.

The projects are grouped into three broad categories based on skill level: Beginner, Intermediate, and Advanced. The first eight projects are perfect for those who have never worked with concrete before. They're

fun and help develop simple skills you can refine. The next eight projects take the simple skills you've learned and apply them in more challenging ways. In some cases you may simply be combining a few simple techniques for one project, whereas in other instances you may be working on skills that take a little practice. Finally, the last eight projects are perfect for when you've got a little experience under your belt.

Flip through the projects, and read through the Materials and Tools lists and the Instructions. Find a project you feel comfortable with—perhaps one that doesn't require a lot of

materials you don't already have around your home. Take into account the work space you're going to use. Is it adequate for the project you're about to undertake? Lay down some plastic, put on a dust mask and a good pair of latex gloves, and you're ready to go.

Other Considerations

Many projects refer to the techniques described in Chapters 2 and 3. Make sure to take the materials and tools needed for those techniques into consideration when deciding which project to start with.

The concrete and slurry mixes needed for each project appear as the first listing in the Materials and Tools section. The mixes are referred to by number and appear on pages 28 through and 30. Work safely and have fun.

Tufa Trough
Designer: Elder G. Jones

Years ago, garden troughs were laboriously chiseled out of blocks of stone. They made the perfect spot to showcase acid-loving plants, and they still do. Prized, moss-covered troughs can be found in antique stores, but they command top dollar, so why not create your own version of this planter at a fraction of the cost? All you do is create a basic form, mix together ingredients you can find at the local home improvement/garden center, and refine the shape with a few simple tools. This trough is actually made from a mix known as hypertufa, not tufa (compressed volcanic ash), but I couldn't resist the alliteration.

MATERIALS & TOOLS

CONCRETE MIX: Mix 7

— Tape measure

— Saw

— ³/₄-inch (1.9 cm) plywood

— Phillips-head screwdriver

— Drywall screws

— Mold release agent

— Plastic work board

— Medium container to mix concrete

— Block of wood

— Trowel

— Putty knife

— Assorted carving tools: sharp kitchen knife, saw blades, etc.

— 2 mil plastic

— Drill with a masonry bit (optional)

— 2 pieces of ¹/₂-inch (1.3 cm) hardwood dowel, or metal rod, 5 inches long (12.7 cm) (optional)

CUTTING LIST FOR THE FORMS

CODE	DESCRIPTION	QTY.	MATERIAL	DIMENSIONS
A	Trough Sides	2	Plywood	10 x 34" (25.4 x 86.4 cm)
B	Trough Ends	2	Plywood	10 x 10" (25.4 x 25.4 cm)
C	Leg Sides	4	Plywood	10 x 10" (25.4 x 25.4 cm)
D	Leg Ends	4	Plywood	10 x 8" (25.4 x 20.3 cm)

INSTRUCTIONS

Creating the Trough Forms

1

Cut the plywood pieces (A, B, C, D).

2

Butt the trough pieces (A, B) to form a rectangle, and screw them together.

3

Butt two leg sides (C) and two leg ends (D) together to form a leg form, and screw the boards together. Repeat with the remaining boards.

Casting the Trough

1

Apply the mold release to the inside of each plywood form.

2

Set the forms on the plastic work board.

3

Mix the concrete and fill each form. Use the small block of wood to tamp or pack the mixture to eliminate air bubbles.

4

Trowel off the tops to level, and let the castings set for six to eight hours.

5

Unscrew and remove the forms.

6

With the putty knife, carve out the inside shape of the trough. Take care not to carve any area too thinly. Carve a drainage hole at the bottom of the trough.

7

With the assorted carving tools, carve the outside of the trough and its legs to the desired shapes. As you work with this material, you'll find it more effective to use a sharp knife to cut edges and surfaces rather than using the scraping tools. However, a saw-toothed blade tool can add a good overall finish texture to the piece. Leave the pieces uncovered and undisturbed overnight (they're quite fragile at this stage).

8

Move the pieces outside, and spray with water. Wrap them in plastic, and cure for two weeks. You may want to wait as long as four weeks before setting the trough up on its legs to allow the material to reach its maximum strength.

9

Set the trough on its legs. For additional stability, use the masonry bit to drill through the trough into each leg. Then pin the trough to the legs with the dowels or metal rods.

Sand-Cast Frame

The surface texture created from this simple casting technique makes the frame look both ancient and contemporary. You don't even need a specialized mold, just a sand pile and a few household items to make a frame for a favorite picture or to prepare a mirror for hanging. The basic instructions can easily be modified to make a decorative wall hanging. In addition to carving and digging designs in the sand to create your relief, press small objects, such as rocks, shells, or pieces of glass, onto the sand's surface, and they will become part of the cast concrete design.

MATERIALS & TOOLS

CONCRETE MIX: Premixed Sand (Topping) Mix, Mortar Mix, or Mix 3

— Low box, larger than the planned frame

— Sand

— Scissors or craft knife

— Ruler

— Corrugated cardboard

— Duct tape

— Try square

— Table knife and spoon

— Assorted wooden blocks

— Mallet or hammer

— Aviator shears

— ¹/₂-inch (1.3 cm) hardware cloth

— Short lengths of 22-gauge wire

— Small container to mix concrete

— Trowel or putty knife

— 2 panel hangers

— 2 mil plastic

— Rasp or file

— Newspaper

— Plastic bag

— 5-minute epoxy

— Photograph or mirror

— Piece of paper

— Picture wire

INSTRUCTIONS

1

Fill the low box with approximately 3 inches (7.6 cm) of sand.

2

Add enough water to the sand so that it packs easily but isn't runny. Tamp the sand firmly until it forms a level surface.

3

Cut four strips of the corrugated cardboard 2 inches (5.1 cm) high to form a rectangle the size of the frame opening (see figure 1).

4

Tape the rectangle together, and wrap the bottom edge with duct tape to waterproof.

5

Square up the rectangle with the try square, and position the rectangle onto the center of the sand. Press it into the sand, like a cookie cutter, to make an indentation as a guide. Set the rectangle aside.

6

With the knife and spoon, carve out the negative of the frame, ³/₄ to 1 inch deep (1.9 to 2.5 cm) in the sand, carefully removing the excess sand (figure 1).

7

Stamp designs with the wooden blocks. Use the mallet to tap the blocks to get a good impression.

8

Reposition the cardboard rectangle into the center of the sand mold so that the edge is embedded in the sand. Additional sand can be packed in the center of the rectangle so that it maintains its shape during the casting (figure 1).

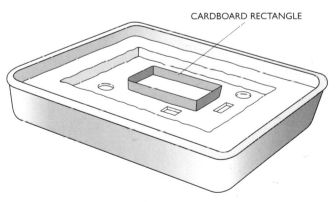

CARDBOARD RECTANGLE

Figure 1

9

Cut four hardware cloth strips with the aviator shears so that, with ends overlapping onto one another, they fit easily within the frame area. Wire them together.

10

Mix the concrete to the consistency of ranch dressing.

11

Pour the concrete into the mold until half full.

12

Use your fingers or a small block of wood to tamp the mixture so that the corners and detail textures are filled.

13

Place the hardware cloth rectangle into the casting, and continue to fill the mold to the top of the sand.

14

Carefully level the concrete with the trowel or putty knife, and insert the two panel hangers 4 inches (10.2 cm) from the top of the frame, in the middle of both sides.

15

Cover the entire box with plastic, and leave undisturbed for 36 hours. Resist the urge to remove the mold any sooner; this is a thin casting, and until there has been ample time for the initial set and cure, the piece will be quite fragile.

16

To remove the casting, scoop out the sand in the middle of the rectangle, and remove the corrugated form. Carefully dig out the sand around the sides so that you can lift the frame out of the sand.

17

Spray the frame with water to remove excess sand. Use the rasp to clean off any edges.

18

To cure, soak about 10 pages of newspaper in water, and wrap the frame. Put the frame into a plastic bag, and leave undisturbed for five days.

19

Unwrap and allow the frame to air dry.

20

After the frame has dried, turn it over on a soft surface so that the hangers are at the sides. Measure the width and height of the frame's opening.

21

To create a backing that will hold the picture or mirror in place, cut two strips out of the corrugated cardboard 1 inch high (2.5 cm). The length of the strips should be the width measurement or the frame opening plus 1½ inches (3.8 cm) (see figure 2).

22.

Cut a rectangle out of the corrugated cardboard the same length as the strips and the same the height of the opening plus 2½ inches (6.4 cm).

23

Generously apply the five-minute epoxy to the cardboard strips. Position them ¼-inch (6 mm) away from the top and bottom of the opening, and centered side to side. Glue the rectangle to the strips and allow to dry thoroughly (see figure 2).

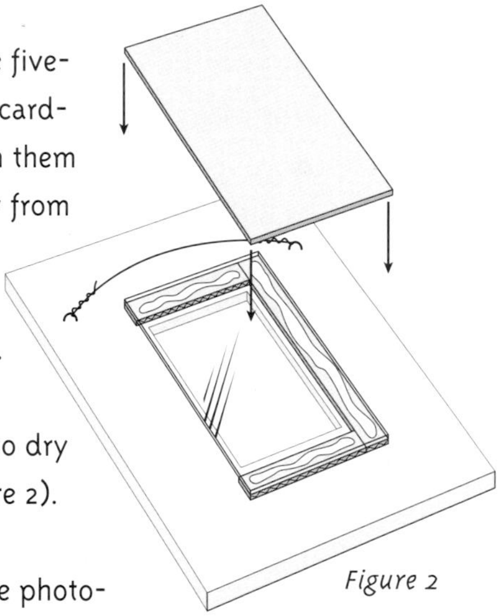

24

Slide the mirror or the photograph into the space created by the cardboard strips between the cardboard rectangle and the frame back. Use a scrap piece of paper to cover the mirror or photo as you slide it in to avoid scratching the surface, and then remove.

25

Attach the picture wire to the panel hangers. Hang the frame from a sturdy hook.

Figure 2

Garden Critters

Inhabitants in my garden inspired the designs for this pathway, but you can choose any idea you like. This project can be broken up into two distinct activities. The first is to prepare your mosaic design; the second is to cast the stepping stones. This is a great garden project to work on even when it isn't good gardening weather, and it's fun to do with kids.

MATERIALS & TOOLS

CONCRETE MIX: Premixed Sand (Topping) Mix, Mortar Mix, or Mix 3
— Reverse-Cast Mosaic materials and tools, page 73

INSTRUCTIONS

1

Select your mold. Use one purchased from a store, or follow the instructions for building a square stepping-stone mold in the Concrete Fossils instructions on page 93.

2

Follow the instructions in Chapter 3 for Reverse-Cast Mosaic, pages 73 through 75.

3

After the stones have cured, place them directly on grass, or recess them in the ground or in decorative rock.

NOTE: If you have more than one mold, it's very useful to prepare a series of designs and then cast them all at the same time. You'll need a plastic-covered work board for each stone, and just one extra board to use to turn the stones over.

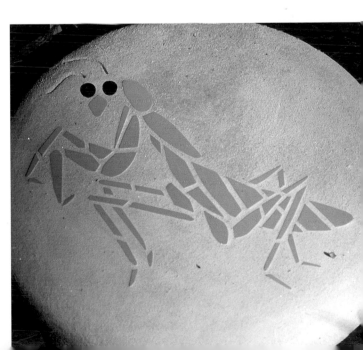

Bookends

Totally chic! Totally retro! These quick and easy bookends will look absolutely fab next to your lava lamp. Not your style? Simply substitute the blue and purple aquarium gravel with natural river rocks, marble chips, or crushed shells to create a completely different look. The texture of these bookends is achieved by scrubbing concrete off the surface to expose the aggregate (in this case, aquarium gravel). This technique, often used on patios and driveways, has been brought down to size for this project.

MATERIALS & TOOLS

CONCRETE MIX: Mix 2

— Saw

— ½-inch-thick (1.3 cm) plywood

— Can opener

— 2 large coffee cans, with tops and bottoms removed

— Paintbrush

— Motor oil, or substitute mold release

— Spray lubricant

— 2 small, plastic-covered work boards

— Sand

— Small container to mix concrete

— Trowel

— Stiff nylon or wire brush

— 2 mil plastic

— Felt or thin sheet of cork

— White glue

INSTRUCTIONS

1

Cut the plywood into two boards that fit snugly inside the center of each can. Each board should also be 1 inch (2.5 cm) taller than the cans.

2

Apply the motor oil to one side of each board with the paintbrush.

3

Lightly apply the spray lubricant inside each can.

4

Position the boards into the center of each can. Make sure the boards are perpendicular to the work surface.

5

Place each can on its own work board.

6

Fill the side of each can that does not have the oil coating on the board with sand. This will hold the board firm as you fill the mold with the concrete.

7

Mix the concrete, and fill the open half of each can, tamping and agitating as you go.

8

Level the top of the castings with the trowel.

9

Let the concrete set up for 10 to 24 hours. You want the castings to be firm, with no water visible when you rub your finger back and forth, but you still should be able to scratch concrete from the surface with your fingernail. If you take your piece out too early, it'll be more fragile, and you'll have to be careful. If you take it out too late, you'll have to scrub harder to expose the aggregate to create the surface texture.

10

To remove the bookends from the molds, pick up the can and push out the sand. Move the center board away from the casting and gently work the can until the piece comes loose.

11

Spray the bookends with water. Use the stiff brush to scrub the surface and remove the concrete, exposing the decorative aggregate. Stop when you're pleased with the surface texture. Spray the bookends periodically as you work to remove the concrete residue.

12

Cover the bookends wtih the plastic, and cure for one week, then air dry for at least three weeks.

13

To finish, glue felt or cork sheeting to the bottom of each bookend so they won't scratch your shelves. Groovy!

Concrete Fossils

Even though these aren't fossils from another geological age, the imprint of leaves gathered on a nature walk or from around your home can create lasting memories. This is the type of project that family members can enjoy doing together. The instructions show a square, but the same technique will work in any shape mold. Create concrete fossils as stepping stones for a path, or to add an interesting accent in your garden.

MATERIALS & TOOLS

CONCRETE MIX: Premixed Sand (Topping) Mix, Mortar Mix, or Mix 3

— Saw

— 5½ linear feet (1.7 m) of 1 x 3 stock*

— 1 linear foot (30 cm) of 2 x 2 stock*

— Drill

— Sandpaper

— Phillips-head screwdriver

— 16 drywall screws, 1¼ inches (3.2 cm) long*

— 2 plastic-covered work boards

— Mold release agent

— Aviator shears

— Reinforcing material

— Flat leaves

— Medium container to mix concrete

— Screed

— Paper or synthetic towels

— Putty knife

— Sponge

— Sharp, pointed knife or straight pin

— Rasp or file (optional)

— Plastic garbage bag

*Quantity listed is for one mold. Multiply the quantity for the number of molds you plan on making.

CUTTING LIST FOR THE SQUARE STEPPING-STONE MOLD

CODE	DESCRIPTION	QTY.	MATERIAL	DIMENSIONS
A	Sides	2	1 x 3 stock	2 x 14" (5.1 x 35.6 cm)
B	Ends	2	1 x 3 stock	2 x 18 1/4" (5.1 x 46.3 cm)
C	Supports	4	2 x 2 stock	2" long (5.1 cm)

INSTRUCTIONS

Building a Square Stepping-Stone Mold (2 x 14 x 14 inches [5.1 x 35.6 x 35.6 cm])

1

Cut the two sides (A), the two ends (B), and the four supports (C), and sand all edges lightly.

2

Predrill two holes into each end of the side pieces (A).

3

Attach two supports (C) to both ends of each side piece (A) (see illustration), and insert the screws from the inside of the sides into the supports.

4

Place the two sides (A) on their edges with the supports facing out. Predrill two holes at each end of the end boards (B). Align the ends to the supports, and attach them with two drywall screws per support, to form the square. These are the screws you'll remove to take the mold apart. Apply the mold release agent to the inside of the mold.

Casting the Fossil

1

With the aviator shears, cut the hardware cloth ½-inch (1.3 cm) smaller than the inside of the mold and set aside.

2

Position the mold on the work board, and arrange the leaves inside the mold, vein side up, as you would like them to appear in the casting.

3

Mix the concrete. Take a small amount, and pat it onto the leaves to anchor them to the plastic work surface. Overlap the applications of the concrete, patting to blend the seams until the bottom of the mold is covered.

4

Complete the casting according to the Reverse Casting instructions on pages 73 through 75, steps 11 through 13.

5

Use the sponge to clean the edge of the mold. You may also need to use the sponge to gently wash away any concrete that has covered the leaves or stems, and to wipe over the rest of the concrete to unify the surface texture.

6

Carefully remove the leaves. Use the sharp knife or straight pin to lift stubborn edges.

7

Remove the mold, and lightly sponge the sides and edges of the casting.

8

Cover the casting with plastic for 24 hours.

9

File the bottom edge of the fossil. Cure the fossil for one week, and then allow it to air dry.

Variation: An easy variation of this project is to cast and finish the top of a mold. Allow the concrete to firm up, and let the surface water evaporate until no longer shiny (approximately 30 to 45 minutes). Then position your pressed leaves firmly into the surface. Allow the casting to sit undisturbed overnight. If you don't want to use leaves, cast and finish the top of the mold as above, and use objects to stamp or a pencil to incise designs (Chapter 3, page 61 through 63). You can also press your hand into the surface until you have a good impression. When doing this, I recommend that you first apply a good coat of hand cream, and wash your hand when finished.

Masonry Planter

This planter was inspired by one I saw, with a hefty price tag on it, at an antique mall. When I asked about it, I learned it had been purchased from an estate sale and had been made by an unknown folk artist. The basic construction technique is really like building a little rock wall. Make this planter special by including some rocks you've gathered on vacations, or simply break up a few bricks like I did here.

MATERIALS & TOOLS

CONCRETE MIX: Premixed Mortar Mix or Mix 3 or 6

— Assorted rocks, pebbles, and broken brick
— Safety goggles
— Masonry hammer
— Small container to mix concrete
— Plastic-covered work board
— Small, round, plastic wastepaper can
— Pointed trowel
— Plastic garbage bag
— Kitchen knife
— Nylon brush
— Muriatic acid (optional)

INSTRUCTIONS

1

Collect assorted rocks and pebbles. With your safety goggles on, use the masonry hammer to break bricks into chunks. Set aside.

2

Mix the concrete to a stiff, smooth, no-slump consistency.

3

On the work board, lay a round bed of concrete approximately 1½ inches (3.8 cm) thick, and 4 inches (10.2 cm) larger in diameter than the wastepaper can.

4

Center the wastepaper can on top of the bed of concrete.

5

Arrange a row of flat rocks on the concrete bed so that they protrude past the outside perimeter of the concrete. Press on the rocks slightly to secure them.

6

With the trowel, place a row of concrete next to the wastepaper can, covering slightly more than half of each embedded rock. Use the point of the trowel to work the concrete in and around the rocks.

7

Select another group of rocks, and arrange them on the new layer of concrete, staggering the arrangement from the first row. Tap lightly to seat the rocks.

8

Continue as if you're building a rock wall around the wastepaper can until you reach the desired height for the planter. For this example, I used six rows of rocks and finished the rim with some of my favorite rocks, arranging them a little closer, and pushing just enough to secure them into the last application of concrete.

9

Cover the planter, including the wastepaper can, with plastic, and leave undisturbed for 24 hours.

10

The next day, carefully remove the wastepaper can by twisting slightly as you pull upward.

11

With the knife, carve a hole in the center of the bottom of the planter for drainage.

12

Spray the planter with water, and cover with plastic for one week.

13

Remove the plastic, and clean the rocks with the nylon brush. Use the muriatic acid to further clean the surface, if desired.

Jazzy Border

Create a garden border that's jazzy in two meanings of the word. Improvise and make it flashy. Start by creating beautiful border bricks, and then throw in some funky found objects to add unexpected contrast. Gather up a variety of elements—lamp parts, bowling balls, machine parts, and other interesting thingamajigs. If you'd prefer a more natural border, try coral, driftwood, rocks, and large shells. Try organizing and rearranging the elements in the grass before you actually try to install it. Pretend you're making music...improvise.

MATERIALS & TOOLS

CONCRETE MIX: Premixed Sand (Topping) Mix, Mortar Mix, or Mix 3

— Saw
— 4 linear feet (1.2 m) of 1 x 6 stock*
— 2 linear feet (61 cm) of 2 x 2 stock*
— Sandpaper
— Drill with ⅛-inch (3 mm) bit
— Phillips-head screwdriver
— 16 drywall screws, 1¼ inches long (3.2 cm)*
— Reverse-Cast Mosaic materials and tools, page 73
— 2 mil plastic
— Rocks, lamp parts, bowling balls, machinery parts, and other found objects (optional)

* Quantity listed is for one brick mold. Multiply the quantity for the number of brick molds you plan to make. You can save time by casting several bricks at once.

CUTTING LIST FOR THE BRICK MOLD

CODE	DESCRIPTION	QTY.	MATERIAL	DIMENSIONS
A	Sides	2	1 x 6 stock	4 x 10" (10.2 x 25.4 cm)
B	Ends	2	1 x 6 stock	4 x 9½" (10.2 x 24.1 cm)
C	Supports	4	2 x 2 stock	4" long (10.2 cm)

INSTRUCTIONS

Building the Brick Mold

1

Cut the wood as specified in the cutting list, and sand all edges lightly to remove any splinters.

2

Attach two supports (C) to both ends of each side piece (A). Use two drywall screws for each support, and screw them in from the inside of the side boards into the supports. Take care to align the supports flush with the edges of the sides (see illustration).

3

Place the two side pieces (A) on their sides with the supports facing out. Align the ends to the supports (C), and attach to the supports with two drywall screws for each support.

4

Repeat for the number of bricks you plan on making at the same time.

Making the Bricks

1

The brick designs are created using the Reverse-Cast Mosaic technique detailed in Chapter 3, pages 73 through 75. The only differences are that the brick mold is different and no work boards are needed. You can work directly on a flat, plastic-covered table.

2

Cure for five days in the plastic, and then air dry.

3

Design your border using the bricks and selected found objects.

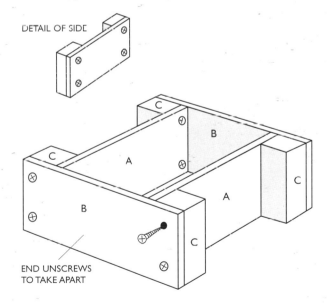

DETAIL OF SIDE

END UNSCREWS TO TAKE APART

Ornamental Sphere

Designer: George E. Adamy

There's something amusing about a large sphere you know is made from concrete but that you can actually pick up. Make your sphere any size you want, from a ping-pong ball to an 8-foot (2.4 m) weather balloon. Relative to its scale, you'll end up with a permanent, lightweight object that can "live" wherever you want it to. This project utilizes the Polyadam Concrete System, which uses portland cement, aggregate, Polyadam II or PII (a high-quality, acrylic, polymer additive), and glass scrim to build up a skin on the ball armature. This system will make an indoor/outdoor, strong yet lightweight, sphere that's waterproof and easily colored.

MATERIALS & TOOLS

CONCRETE MIX: Mix 10; Slurry Mix 16

— Sphere, any size, any material

— Container big enough to hold sphere

— Polyadam Concrete System Applied over a Poly-styrene Foam Form materials and tools, page 58

— Acrylic artist paints (optional)

— Metallic waxes (optional)

INSTRUCTIONS

1

Select any size sphere made from any material: rubber, plastic, paper, clay, wax, wood, plastic, cloth, etc.

2

Set the sphere in a container that will support it with half or more of the surface exposed to work on.

3

Cut the glass scrim into small strips or squares.

4

Brush a layer of PII onto the ball. Use two layers of PII if using a sphere made out of a porous material such as polystyrene foam, foam rubber, paper, or cloth.

5

Mix a stiff concrete, and apply a thin layer to an area of the ball slightly larger than the size of the scrim you've cut.

6

Immediately press the scrim into the concrete. If the concrete begins to slip, you either have too loose a mix, you applied it too thickly, or you moved the armature before it has set up.

7

Only one-half of the ball is worked on until the cement has time to set (as little as 20 minutes). After the first half has set, carefully rotate your piece, and continue to cover the entire ball, overlapping the scrim.

8

On medium-sized balls (4 to 6 inches [10.2 to 15.2 cm] in diameter), add a second layer of light/medium scrim and cover. On medium/large sized balls (8 to 16 inches [20.3 to 40.6 cm] in diameter), add a second layer of scrim, this time heavy-duty. On heroic-sized balls (2 to 8 feet [.6 to 2.4 m] in diameter), use two layers of heavy scrim. On ping-pong balls and smaller, no scrim is necessary, but make the cement thicker.

9

After you've completed covering the sphere, or you've finished a work session, cover the piece with plastic for 24 hours to cure.

10

The next day, use the rasp or block to smooth the surface.

11

Once the piece has received the suggested layers of glass scrim for reinforcement, surface textures can be added with additional application of the concrete system by brushing on a coat of the PII, using the slurry, and by applying the concrete to achieve the desired effect. Repeat step 9.

12

The sphere shown here has been colored with acrylic paints and metallic waxes. You can do the same, or choose one of the other techniques described in Chapter 3: Surface Treatments.

Note: Glass scrim and PII can be mail-ordered. See page 143 for ordering information.

Years ago, artist George E. Adamy proposed a project for the Artpark in Lewiston, New York, near Niagara Falls. His dream was to carve large polystyrene balls, cover them with the Polyadam Concrete System, paint them with the U.S. and Canadian flags, and set them free in the Niagara River to traverse the rapids and then cascade over the falls. The whole event would be taped from a helicopter. The proposal was turned down, but Adamy would still like the opportunity to do it.

Birdbath

The first object I ever created in concrete was a birdbath. After that, I was hooked. What I learned through problem-solving the base construction has led me to develop forming techniques that I've been able to adapt for a wide range of structures. I've taught weekend birdbath workshops in my studio for more than 10 years, and I've seen hundreds of students create their own birdbaths. The beauty of this process is that there has never been any two alike. Individual style, sense of form, and color are combined each time to create a unique piece.

MATERIALS & TOOLS

CONCRETE MIX: Premixed Sand (Topping) Mix, Mortar Mix, or Mix 3; Slurry Mix 14

You'll need the tools and materials listed for the following techniques:

— Sand Casting and Bowl Connection (pages 37 through 40)

— Simple Column Armature and Column Connection (pages 41 through 43).

— Desired surface treatment (Chapter 3)

INSTRUCTIONS

1

To make the base form of the bowl for your birdbath, follow the instructions in Chapter 2: Sand Casting and Bowl Connection, pages 37 through 40. Don't make the bowl too deep—you don't want the birds to drown.

2

To make the base form for the pedestal base, follow the instructions in Chapter 2, Simple Column Armature and Column Connection, pages 41 through 43.

3

To add the final layer of concrete to your base forms and embellish the surfaces, follow the instructions for Surface Treatments in Chapter 3. This birdbath was completed using the embedding techniques described on pages 76 through 77 (the strip of grass on the base of the birdbath shown on the previous page is actually an embedded mirror).

4

To install your birdbath, place the pedestal base on a level spot. Insert the cup stem of the bowl into the base. Fill the bowl with water, and sit back and wait for the birds. In grassy areas, I like to place the base on a precast concrete stepping stone that has a diameter slightly larger than the foot. That way the decoration on the foot doesn't get covered with growing grass, and the lawnmower doesn't hit my birdbath when the grass get cuts.

Construction Timeframe

Constructing a birdbath might take you one or more weekends depending on how intensely you work. In the workshops I teach, we develop the elements in the following sequence:

1

Cast the bowl Friday night.

2

Make the pedestal armature and apply the concrete Saturday morning.

3

Embed the inside of the bowl Saturday afternoon.

4

Embed the pedestal base Sunday morning and afternoon.

5

Embed the back of the bowl later Sunday afternoon.

This is a very intense production schedule, but by doing the pieces in this order, the concrete has ample time to set firmly before moving on to the next step. You can easily approach this project in shorter work sessions to complete a birdbath over a couple of weeks.

Tufa Planter

Designer: Elder G. Jones

Some artists and craftsmen limit themselves to certain materials or techniques to create their work. Out of these limitations can come a lifetime of explorations and variations. This hypertufa planter is another approach to form development. The legs, or feet, are incorporated within the casting of the body of the planter. How many styles of planters can you come up with?

MATERIALS & TOOLS

CONCRETE MIX: Mix 7

— 4 pieces of ¾-inch (1.9 cm) plywood, 14 x 16 inches (35.6 x 40.6 cm)

— Phillips-head screwdriver

— Drywall screws

— Mold release agent

— Plastic-covered work board

— Sand

— Medium container to mix concrete

— Block of wood

— Small cardboard box, approximately 8 inches (20.3 cm) square

— Plastic grocery bag

— Trowel

— Putty knife

— Assorted carving tools: sharp kitchen knife, saw blades, etc.

— 2 mil plastic

INSTRUCTIONS

1

Butt the sides of the four plywood pieces to make a square, and screw them together.

2

Apply the mold release agent to the inside of the form, and set the form on the plastic-covered work board.

3

In the center of the form, pack approximately 2 inches of wet sand in the shape of a cross. Each end of the cross must touch the sides of the form. The empty spaces left in the corners will form the legs of the planter. Make the spaces larger than you actually want 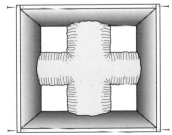 the finished legs to be so you have extra material to shape during the carving process.

4

Mix the concrete and begin to fill the form, starting with the leg spaces. Use the small block of wood to tamp the mixture into the spaces.

5

Once the legs are filled, continue to fill the form up to 3 inches (7.6 cm) for the bottom of the planter, tamping as you go.

6

Put the small cardboard box into the plastic bag, and arrange the plastic so that the folds and wrinkles are minimized. Center it into the casting. Fill the box with damp sand so it holds its shape.

7

Continue to fill the space between the form and the cardboard box, which will be approximately 3 inches (7.6 cm), tamping as you go.

8

Trowel off the top to level, and let the casting set for six to eight hours.

9

Unscrew the form and remove it from the casting. Remove the inside box by first removing the sand and then lifting the plastic bag. Some of the plastic may stick into the cast, but it can be carved out later.

10

Follow steps 6 and 7 from the Tufa Trough on page 85. This material is fragile. Don't try to pick up the piece or turn it over. Always move your work board rather than the piece. When you shape the legs, carve them the best you can, using smaller tools so you can reach under and around the form more easily. Leave the finished piece uncovered and undisturbed overnight.

11

The next day, move it outside to spray with water. Wrap the planter in plastic to cure for two weeks.

Pacific Rim Lantern

Reminiscent of the stone lanterns that light the way in Japanese gardens, this concrete version can be styled using easy-to-find items that may already be in your garage or basement. A 3-gallon (11.4 L) nursery planter, a round dish pan, a large pot lid or flat metal lamp shade can be adapted to use as molds to cast the lantern parts. If you prepare all of your molds for this project ahead of time, you can cast the whole lantern at the same time. The polystyrene foam insulation can be cut to any shape and size.

MATERIALS & TOOLS

CONCRETE MIX: Premixed Mortar Mix or Mix 1 or 2

- Sharp knife
- 2-inch polystyrene foam insulation
- Duct tape
- Round plastic bowl or dish pan (base mold)
- Spray lubricant
- Large plastic planter, 3 gallons (11.4 L) (body mold)
- Plastic planter, the same height as the large plastic planter, but 4 inches (10.2 cm) smaller in diameter
- Round flat form: metal lamp shade, wok lid, or large lid from a pot (top mold)
- 2-liter plastic soda or juice bottle (finial mold)
- Utility knife
- 1 round rock
- Container to hold finial mold
- Medium container to mix concrete
- 4 plastic garbage bags
- Rasp
- Small wire brush
- Candle

INSTRUCTIONS

1

For the base of the lantern, use the sharp knife to cut four small arches from the polystyrene insulation (see figure 1), and tape them to the inside of the round dish pan with the flat edge of each arch even with the rim of the container (see figure 2). These will help form the legs of the base.

Figure 1

2

Spray the inside of the dish pan with the spray lubricant, and set aside.

3

For the body of the lantern, use the sharp knife to cut four window shapes from the polystyrene insulation (see figure 3), and set aside.

4

Spray the inside of the large plastic planter and the outside of the smaller planter with the spray lubricant, and set aside.

5

For the top of the lantern, spray the round, flat form you selected with the spray lubricant, and set aside.

6

For the finial, cut the plastic bottle in half with the utility knife, and discard the bottom half of the bottle.

7

Place the rock in the neck of the bottle so it acts like a stopper. Place the finial mold in the container to hold it upright during casting.

8

Now that the molds are ready, mix the concrete to a firm, no-slump consistency.

9

For the base, press the concrete into the bowl, tamping firmly to get rid of any air bubbles. The bottom of the bowl should be filled to about 3 inches thick (7.6 cm). As you work up the sides, be sure to fill around the arches as you go. Build the sides up about 2 inches thick (5.1 cm). Set aside.

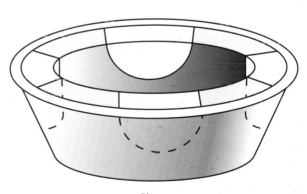

Figure 2

10

For the body, tamp 2 inches (5.1 cm) of concrete into the bottom of the large planter. Center the smaller planter so there is an equal space all the way around to create a ring approximately 2 inches wide (5.1 cm).

11

Fill in the ring-shaped space between the two planters until you get to where you'd like to place the windows, approximately 3 inches (7.6 cm).

12

Place the polystyrene window shapes into the ringed area so they're equally spaced between the two planters. Continue to tamp the concrete into the ring area, between the window forms, covering them as you fill the body mold to the top (see figure 3).

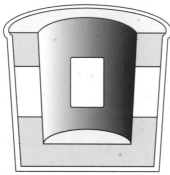

Figure 3

13

For the lantern top, firmly pack concrete into the round, flat form to create an even 2-inch (5.1 cm) layer.

14

For the finial, with the rock in place as a stopper, pack concrete into the bottle about 3 to 4 inches (7.6 to 10.2 cm).

15

Cover all the forms with the plastic bags, and leave undisturbed for a minimum of 24 hours.

16

Carefully remove the pieces from the molds. In some cases, you may need to cut the mold apart to remove the piece.

17

Pull the smaller planter out from the middle of the body casting, and remove the window shapes. Also remove the arches from the base mold.

18

Clean up the castings using the rasp and sharp knife to smooth any edges. Use the wire brush to remove any polystyrene foam that may have remained in the casting.

19

Hose each piece with water, wrap them back up in the plastic bags, and allow them to cure for at least five days.

20

To assemble, position the base on a level surface. Center the body with the opening upward, and place a candle inside. Center the top and then the finial.

Frog Fountain

There's nothing quite so soothing as the sound of running water, whether it's in the garden or on your patio or deck. Wherever it is you go to be still and relax, this charming fountain will help enhance those reflective moments. The basic components of a fountain are all here: the water reservoir, an element that both conceals the pump and spouts the water, and a stand to hold the reservoir. Make a fountain like this playful frog, or alter the components to personalize the design. The principles remain the same. Once you've created your elements and adjusted your water flow, all that remains is for you to sit back and enjoy.

MATERIALS & TOOLS

CONCRETE MIX: Premixed Sand (Topping) Mix, Mortar Mix, or Mix 3; Slurry Mix 14

— Sand Casting materials and tools (page 37)

— Embedding materials and tools (page 76)

— Caulk gun

— Construction caulk adhesive

— 3 polystyrene foam ring shapes

— Rasp or small wire brush

— Permanent marker

— Aviator shears

— $\frac{1}{2}$-inch (1.3 cm) hardware cloth

— Tape measure

— 6-inch (15.2 cm) pieces of 22-gauge galvanized or stainless-steel wire

— $1\frac{1}{4}$-inch (3.2 cm) roofing nails

— Thin-set mortar adhesive, polymer fortified (optional)

— $\frac{1}{4}$-inch (6 mm) hardware cloth

— Brass tube fitting

— 10-inch (25.4 cm) piece of 22-gauge galvanized wire

— Masking tape

— Duct tape

— 2 mil plastic

— Small adjustable, submersible statuary pump

— Flexible plastic tubing, sized to fit the pump and brass fitting

INSTRUCTIONS

Forming the Reservoir or Bowl

I

To make the base form of the fountain reservoir or bowl, follow the instructions in Chapter 2: Sand Casting, pages 37 through 39. Keep in mind that the shape of the bowl must be deep enough for the pump and large enough that the water spray or movement is contained.

2

The decoration on this fountain bowl utilized the embedding technique, pages 76 through 77. It's always best to prepare the materials for your design before you start to embed. Designs can be positioned on your bowl form, before you add the final layer of concrete, to get a good idea of how the final piece will look. Move the pieces off the base form before you start to embed.

3

Cure the completed piece for five days.

Forming the Base

I

To form the base that will hold the bowl or reservoir, refer to Chapter 2 and the Column Armature examples as you work on the following construction.

2

With the caulk adhesive, glue the three polystyrene rings together to form a short column.

3

The top edge of the column form should be beveled toward the center to hold the bowl. Use the rasp or small wire brush to shape the bevel.

4

With the permanent marker, make two tracings of the column onto the ½-inch (1.3 cm) hardware cloth. Cut out the patterns with the aviator shears. Set the rings of mesh aside.

5

Measure the height and circumference of the polystyrene foam column. Cut out a strip of hardware cloth that is the height by two times the circumference, plus 2 more inches (5.1 cm).

6

Wrap the hardware cloth strip around the column form twice, and secure with the pieces of 22-gauge wire.

7

Measure the inside circumference of the column form. Cut out a strip of hardware cloth that is the height by two times the circumference of the inside circle, and secure with wire. It helps to use roofing nails as "tacks" to hold the hardware cloth in place. Press them through the mesh into the polystyrene foam. The nails can be left in while you form over the armature.

8

Secure the rings of mesh to both sides of the form using the wire along both the inside and outside edges. Cut once through the mesh ring that goes on the beveled edge to make it easier to position.

9

Mix the concrete and slurry. Slurry the polystyrene foam and mesh form. Apply the concrete to the top, bottom, and sides of the mesh to completely cover the form. Cover with plastic overnight.

10

The next day, hose the piece with water and refine the edges with the rasp, if needed.

11

Cure the base, then mosaic the rocks to the base using the polymer fortified, thin-set mortar adhesive. Use the same concrete mixture to grout so that all the pieces work together. Refer to Chapter 3: Mosaic, pages 67 through 73.

12

Cure the completed piece for five days.

Forming the Frog

1

Using the ¼-inch (6 mm) hardware cloth, create a small bowl-like form that will be the basic form for your frog. Make sure that the initial form is large enough to cover or conceal the pump and the tubing. Build a simple armature, adding small pieces of folded mesh to indicate the legs, and use the wire to attach them to the form.

2

Wrap a 10-inch (25.4 cm) piece of wire tightly around the brass fitting. Insert the fitting into the armature in the mouth area. Fasten the ends of the wire into the armature so that the fitting feels secure.

3

Cover the ends of the fitting with masking tape so that it doesn't accidentally get filled with concrete.

4

Cut short pieces of duct tape, about 3 inches long (7.6 cm), and cover the inside of the mesh form with the tape. Overlap the tape so that it creates a solid surface or barrier on the inside of the form. Make sure that at least ¾ inch (1.9 cm) of the brass fitting is extended past the duct tape surface. The hose for the pump will be attached to this end, so it must remain accessible through the concreting process.

5

Mix the concrete, and apply it to the outside of the armature, taking care not to press so hard that it pushes the duct tape off the inside of the mesh. Press the concrete into the folded mesh leg forms. Be careful not to build up too much material around the part of the brass fixture that is protruding out of the mouth area.

6

After the first coat of concrete, this piece will NOT closely resemble a frog. Cover with plastic and leave overnight.

7

The next day, spray with water, and refine the shape with the rasp as needed.

8

Mix the concrete and slurry. Refer to Chapter 2: Direct Modeling, pages 55 through 57. Begin to build up the basic frog form. It's unlikely that you'll be able to finalize the frog with this second application.

9

Repeat steps 6 and 7 for the third application.

10

If you're planning to embed any decoration, do so on the third and final application. Cover with plastic when you're finished working. Refer to Chapter 3: Embedding, pages 76 through 77.

11

The next day, refine your form with the rasp as needed. Make sure that at least 1/8 inch (3 mm) of the brass fitting is still protruding from the mouth; file if necessary.

12

Turn the piece upside down, and remove the duct tape and the masking tape. Make sure that at least 3/4 inch (1.9 cm) of the brass fitting is still exposed. Cover the piece in plastic, and allow it to cure for three to five days.

Assembling the Fountain

1

Cut a short piece of flexible tubing that fits onto the brass fitting in the frog and onto the pump. Put the tube on the fitting.

2

Position the bowl onto the base and place the pump into the bowl.

3

Place the pump cord over the side of the bowl to the inside ring of the base. Lift the base slightly so you can pull the plug and remaining cord out from the inside of the column base.

4

Attach the flexible tubing to the pump.

5

If necessary, lift the base and pull on the pump cord so that the pump is in position and the cord is pulled snugly around the edge of the bowl into and under the base.

6

Once everything is in position, fill the bowl with water and plug in your fountain. If the frog is shooting water out of your bowl, adjust the level of your pump or reposition the frog.

7

Once you're pleased with your water flow, the cord can be camouflaged with an artful arrangement of rocks.

Dee Oh Gee

Okay, so walking the dog just became a little more difficult, but he's so easy to clean up after, and he always has a grin. Your animal doesn't have to be a dog. In fact, these basic instructions can be used to fashion any sort of creature, real or imagined. You might get so hooked on making animals that you'll decide to open your own pet store or zoo.

MATERIALS & TOOLS

CONCRETE MIX: Premixed Mortar Mix or Mix 5 and Mix 3; Slurry Mix 14

— Simple Animal Armature materials and tools (page 44)

— 36 linear feet (11 m) of rebar

— Desired Surface Treatment materials and tools (Chapter 3)

— ¼-inch (6 mm) dowel, sharpened to a point

CUTTING LIST FOR THE ARMATURE REBAR

CODE	DESCRIPTION	QTY.	LENGTHS
A	Legs	4	22" (55.9 cm)
B	Sides	4	20" (50.8 cm)
C	Top of Head	2	20" (50.8 cm)
D	Front & Back	4	9" (22.9 cm)
E	Tail Support	3	12" (30.5 cm)
F	Back Leg Support	2	8" (20.3 cm)
G	Head Support	1	15" (38.1 cm)

INSTRUCTIONS

1

Cut the rebar to designated lengths, and file the cut edges to remove the burrs.

2

Follow the instructions in Chapter 2: Simple Animal Armature, pages 44 through 47.

3

The final application of concrete should accommodate your surface treatment (refer to Chapter 3 to explore your options) and include the definition of the eyes, nose, and mouth. (Refer to Direct Modeling, pages 55 through 57). Consider the surface you want on your sculpture. The hair of this dog was incised into the final layer of concrete with the sharpened piece of dowel and allowed to set before wrapping in plastic so the texture wouldn't get flattened. Say "Woof!"

Gazing Ball Stand

Gazing balls, those wonderful, colored mirror spheres, have recently regained popularity as a garden orna-
ment. As I understand it, they first became popular in the Victorian era and again in 1950s' suburbs where
lawn and garden space was limited. The glassy ball reflects a smallish flower bed, much like a fun house
mirror, giving one the impression the bed is bigger than it actually is. To create a standout stand, match the
proportions of the base to the gazing ball you're using (gazing balls are available in a wide range of sizes),
and coordinate the colored tiles or glass for embedding.

MATERIALS & TOOLS

CONCRETE MIX: Premixed Sand (Topping) Mix, Masonry Mix, or Mix 3; Slurry Mix 14

You'll need the tools and materials listed for the following techniques:

– Polystyrene Foam as a Column Armature (page 43)

– Embedding (page 76) (optional)

– Incising (page 62) (optional)

– Gazing ball

– Muriatic acid (optional)

– Floral clay or beeswax

INSTRUCTIONS

1

To make the base form (the conical stand), follow the instructions in Chapter 2: Polystyrene Foam as a Column Armature, page 43.

2

To add the final layer of concrete to the stand and embellish the surface, follow the instructions for Surface Treatments in Chapter 3. The glassy centered swirls on the stand's surface are a combination of embedding, page 76 and incising, page 62. The tile strips at the bottom were cut by a tile saw, but also could have been formed using a contractor's style cutter.

3

Cure the finished piece for five days, and then allow to air dry.

4

To install your gazing ball stand, soften enough beeswax or floral clay in your hand to make a ¼-inch (6 mm) coil. Place it at the inside top edge of the opening of the stand. Set the gazing ball onto the coil and push firmly to ensure a good bond.

Ancient Carving

There's an archeological quality about this carving material: anything you carve from it looks as if it's just been dug up from an ancient ruin. The stone color of the concrete, the naturally occurring air bubbles, and the reflective bits of mica from the vermiculite, combine to give this cast material the look of ancient stone. The day you take the block out of your form, it'll carve like butter! Develop your details as the cast material hardens over the few days you work on it.

MATERIALS & TOOLS

CONCRETE MIX: Mix 8

— Container to cast form*

— Plastic garbage bag

— Container to mix concrete

— Assorted wood chisels

— Lightweight mallet or hammer

— Surform rasp

— Assorted flat and curved rasps

— Assorted riffler rasps

— Sharp kitchen knife

— Wire brush

— Handsaw (optional)

* You can cast your block in almost any type of container. I used a 2½ gallon (9.5 L) bucket for this head. Waxed milk containers work well for smaller pieces, or you can line a cardboard box with a plastic bag.

INSTRUCTIONS

1

Line the container in which you're casting with the plastic garbage bag. Arrange the plastic as flat against the container as you can, eliminating as many creases as possible.

2

Mix the concrete, and pour it into the container. Vibrate the container by tapping the sides to eliminate most of the air bubbles, but don't overdo it, or the vermiculite will begin to separate from the mixture. Leave the casting undisturbed for 12 to 24 hours.

3

Remove the casting from the container. If you used a cardboard box, it can be cut away from the casting. If you used a plastic container, try gathering up the plastic bag and pulling it out of the container.

4

After you've removed the form, pull the plastic bag off the casting. Don't worry if small pieces of plastic are stuck in the casting, these will be removed as you carve.

5

Refer to Chapter 2: Carving Basics, pages 50 through 55.

6

Don't try to define delicate areas or to proceed with detail or surface texture at this point. The material is still too soft. Once you've blocked out the basic form, cover the emerging sculpture with plastic, and wait until the next day.

7

As you return to the piece, you'll see that the casting has continued to cure and is harder. Continue to carve and develop your sculpture as you experiment with your tools. If the chisel has left irregular marks in the surface, smooth them over with the surform rasp. Details can be refined with the help of the riffler rasp or sharp knife. If your piece has dried between work sessions, wet it down with water. This will keep dust to a minimum.

8

When you've finished your carving, spray it with water to remove the dust. This will also expose airholes on the surface, which will give your carving a more natural stonelike appearance.

Bluebird/Pink House

Combine your favorite concrete-forming techniques with funky found objects to create a mixed-media totem. Don't be concerned if the stacked objects don't tell a clear story. If "experiment with the juxtaposition of objects to create a more formal composition" sounds a bit too artsy, then let me put it another way: Be playful as you create the shapes, and experiment with their arrangement.

MATERIALS & TOOLS

CONCRETE MIXES: Premixed Sand (Topping) Mix, Mortar Mix, or Mix 2; Mix 3; Mix 10; Slurry: Mixes 14 and 15

— Handsaw

— Tape measure

— 1-inch-diameter (2.5 cm) PVC pipe

— Masking tape

— Small and medium-sized containers to mix concrete

— Plastic-covered work boards

— Level

— 2 mil plastic

— Sharp knife

— File or rasp

— Container to mix slurry

— Paintbrush

— Shells, glass gems, and other frost-resistant materials

— Sanding disc to attach to 4½-inch (11.4 cm) grinder or power drill (optional)

— 8-inch (20.3 cm) polystyrene ball

— 3-inch (7.6 cm) common nails

— Caulk gun

— Construction caulk adhesive

— Light/medium glass scrim

— Polymer-fortified thin-set adhesive

— Polymer-fortified sanded grout

— Adapting a Polystyrene Waste Mold for a Totem Constucton materials and tools (page 36)

— Screwdriver

— Small wire brush or riffler rasp

— ½-inch (1.3 cm) hardware cloth

— Stiff nylon scrub brush

— Drill with ¼-inch (6 mm) drill bit

— Color pigment

— Trowel

— ¼-inch (6 mm) bolt, 2 inches long (5.1 cm), with nut

— ¾-inch (1.9 cm) heavy, galvanized pipe, long enough for finished totem

— Optional elements: found metal, ceramic or glass objects

INSTRUCTIONS

Totem Base

1

Cut a piece of PVC pipe 20 inches (50.8 cm) long .

2

Cover the ends of the PVC pipe with masking tape.

3

Mix concrete mix 3. Stand the pipe in the middle of the plastic-covered work board, and shape the concrete into a cone around it. Add concrete as long as it will hold its form without sliding. Check the pipe with the level to make sure it's vertical and true. If the pipe leans, your totem will lean.

4

Cover with plastic, and leave undisturbed until the concrete sets. After it sets, use the sharp knife or file to refine the shape as needed.

5

Mix slurry mix 14 and concrete mix 3. Add additional layers of concrete until you've reached the desired form.

6

Prepare the shells or other materials you want to use for the surface decoration. Follow the instructions for embedding, pages 76 through 77.

7

Remove the masking tape from the pipe, and use the saw to trim the pipe even with the top of the cone. Try sawing the pipe as close as you can without damaging the piece, and then use the file to get the pipe flush. The sanding disc attached to a drill or grinder makes this step easier.

Gem Sphere

1

Cut a 10-inch (25.4 cm) piece of PVC pipe.

2

Cut the 8-inch (20.3 cm) polystyrene ball in half with the handsaw, and follow the instructions for Adapting a Polystyrene Foam Core for a Totem Construction, pages 49 through 50.

3

Apply one layer of the polymer-fortified concrete system as described on pages 58 through 60, cutting the light/medium scrim into 3-inch (7.6 cm) squares. Allow to cure overnight.

4

Trim the pipe to extend out the height of the glass gems or other material you plan to use to mosaic the sphere.

5

Mosaic the surface, applying the material with the thin-set adhesive. Refer to Chapter 3: Mosaic, pages 67 through 73.

6

Allow the adhesive to set overnight, and grout according to directions on pages 72 through 73.

Casting the Bird

1

Follow the instructions for Adapting a Polystyrene Waste Mold for a Totem Construction, pages 36 through 37. Use concrete mix 2.

2

Take outside and spray with water, rubbing the surface with the nylon brush to expose the aggregate. Refer to this process in the Bookends project, page 90.

3

Trim the pipe as described in step 7 of Totem Base.

Pink House (or other top piece)

1

Form your top piece out of polystyrene foam.

2

Refer to Adapting a Polystyrene Core for a Totem Construction, pages 49 through 50, but modify how you inset the pipe.

3

Cut a section of PVC pipe that is two-thirds the length of the piece. Drill a hole straight through both sides of the pipe and insert the bolt and nut. This will keep the support pipe from pushing through the top of your piece.

4

The opening of the pipe should be at the bottom of the top piece. The angle of the pipe in the piece will determine the angle at which the piece will sit on the totem.

5

Mix slurry mix 15 and concrete mix 10. Add the pigment, if desired.

6

Apply the concrete with the trowel to achieve a stucco appearance; pretend you're icing a cake.

7

Allow the surface moisture to evaporate before covering loosely with plastic. You want the piece to cure, but you don't want water to condense and drip on the pigmented surface until it has set up.

Assembling Your Totem

1

Make your final selection of elements, and think about how they'll be arranged—the order you'll stack them.

2

Use the tape measure to measure the length of pipe in each section by measuring the inside of the pipes. Stack the found objects you plan to use to determine their length. You may want to use sections of copper or galvanized pipe as spacers between objects. Include those lengths as you add all the measurements together.

3

Cut your support pipe to the length of the measurements' total.

4

Do a trial stacking. You might want to rearrange some of your elements or put washers between objects. Position the base, insert the pipe, and slide the elements over the pipe. If there's a space between your top element and the object below, cut your pipe shorter. If the length of pipe that is left as you position your top piece is less than half the total height of the top piece, you may want to cut a longer piece of pipe.

For a more permanent outdoor installation, consider setting an 18-inch (45.7 cm) piece of pipe into a concrete footing in the ground, making sure that it is true vertical. Cut the support pipe the length of the totem, plus the depth of the footing pipe. Position the base piece over the footing hole, and insert the pipe. Carefully slide the other elements over the pipe into position.

Rousseau Relief Planter

Designer: Elder G. Jones

Designer Elder Jones's carvings are reminiscent of jungle scenes from paintings by Henri Rousseau. Low levels of stylized fronds and foliage undulate in soft patterns over his carved bas-relief planters. Maybe you're more influenced by industrial motifs and want to carve more angular forms, or perhaps even illustrate some sort of story. Whatever idea has germinated for you can come full bloom as you begin carving. The color variations in the planters pictured are achieved by adding pigments to the concrete mixtures.

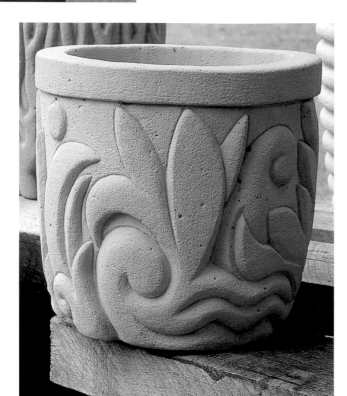

MATERIALS & TOOLS

CONCRETE MIX: Premixed Sand (Topping) Mix or Mix 4
— 2 sheets of galvanized sheet metal
— 2 or 3 small C-clamps
— Thin rope
— Wet Carving materials and tools (page 52)
— 22-gauge galvanized wire
— Plastic planter or food container
— Wood block
— Plastic bag
— Sand
— Sharp kitchen knife
— Plastic garbage bag

INSTRUCTIONS

1

Roll the galvanized sheet metal to the largest outside measurement of your planter and clamp it. Use the thin rope to secure the bottom portion of the mold (see illlustration).

2

Place the plastic work board and clamped sheet metal onto the lazy Susan on your work surface.

3

Prepare the inner form with the second piece of galvanized metal. Roll it to a diameter that is 8 inches (20.3 cm) smaller than the outside form and slightly conical in shape (or smaller at the bottom than the top).

4

Use a small clamp to secure the top, and use the wire to hold the lower portion in place (see illustration).

5

Find a flexible plastic planter or food container that fits snugly in the bottom of the metal cone. Set aside.

6

If you're using the premixed sand mix, first sift the dry ingredients through a window screen to remove any large particles. Mix the concrete.

7

Fill the bottom 3 inches (7.6 cm) of the mold. Tamp it with the wood block.

8

Position the inner form, with the plastic container in place, onto the center of the partially filled form.

9

Place the plastic bag into the center of the inner form, and fill it with damp sand to help the form retain its shape (see illustration).

10

Fill the space between the inner and outer forms, tamping with the wood block as you go. If the bottom rope is not tight enough, adjust the angle of the sides of the outer form by loosening the clamp and repositioning it.

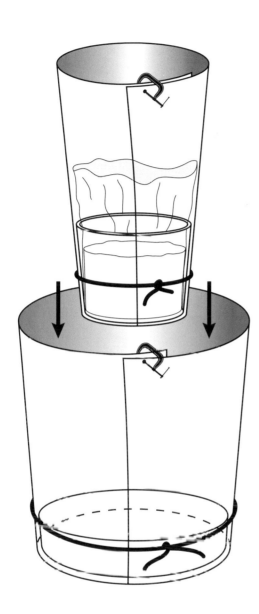

II

Let the casting set three to four hours.

I2

Pull out the plastic bag with the sand, remove the plastic container, and unclamp the inner piece of sheet metal. Roll the metal in slightly, pulling it away from the casting. The bottom wire will still be in the concrete, but you'll remove it later.

I3

Untie the rope that was holding the bottom of the outside piece of sheet metal. Remove the clamp, and carefully remove the metal.

I4

Refine the inside of the planter first, taking into account how deep you want to make your outside relief. Don't carve out too much. Scoop and scrape to level the sides, and remove the wire that was left in the concrete from the inside piece of sheet metal.

I5

Work on the basic silhouette of the planter; do you want the sides straight, or should it taper in at the bottom? Rough out the silhouette with the sharp knife.

I6

With one of the saw blade pieces, scrape the entire form to remove any remaining residue from the surface. Smooth the entire surface slightly with a finer saw-tooth tool or flat edge.

I7

With a sharp, pointed tool, lightly scratch your design into the surface. There's no erasing here, so "lightly" is the operative term.

I8

Refer to Chapter 2: Wet Carving, pages 52 through 54, for tips on how to use the carving tools as you carve the planter. Refine the design with each rotation until you've finished.

I9

Leave the carved planter uncovered and undisturbed overnight.

20

The next day, take the piece outside and hose it down to remove any debris from the surface. Cure for one week by hosing with water several times a day or by wrapping in a wet cloth and covering with plastic.

Little Lady Fountain

Folk artists have crafted wonderfully stylized figures as guardians, politicians, and religious figures in eccentric gardens all over the world. Who can you construct to inhabit your yard or garden? This little lady, who watches wistfully in a gathering of zinnias, also includes a simple self-contained fountain in her over-scaled hat.

Having the arms close to the body requires additional reinforcing materials without the structural concerns of an extended reach. In fact, this figure was developed as a variation on a simple column armature. Like the Frog Fountain on page 107, there are three parts to this piece: the body (the base that holds the reservoir), the hat, and the crown (conceals the pump). You'll construct the little lady's figure first; it's the primary element. You'll want the hat shape to relate to her.

MATERIALS & TOOLS

CONCRETE MIX: Premixed Sand (Topping) Mix, Mortar Mix, or Mix 3; Slurry Mix 14
You'll need the materials and tools listed for the following techniques:

- Simple Column Armature, page 41
- Column Connection, page 42
- Direct Modeling, page 56
- Incising, page 62
- Embedding, page 76
- Sand Casting, page 37
- Connector Bowl, page 39
- $1/4$-inch (6 mm) hardware cloth
- $41/2$-inch (11.4 cm) grinder with masonry wheel
- $1/2$-inch (1.3 cm) flexible hose
- Spray water bottle
- 2-inch (5.1 cm) diameter PVC pipe
- Small, plastic mixing bowl
- Spray lubricant
- Roll of alkali-resistant fiberglass mesh
- Drill with $1/2$-inch (1.3 cm) masonry bit
- Brass fitting or fountain nozzle
- Small, adjustable, submersible pump

INSTRUCTIONS

Forming the body

1

Determine how tall you want your base to be. This little lady stands 40 inches (101.6 cm) high.

2

Refer to Simple Column Armature with Column Connector, Chapter 2, pages 41 through 42, and follow steps 1 through 8. Also follow steps 1 and 2 of Column Connection.

3

Take two 6 x 10-inch (15.2 x 25.4 cm) pieces of $1/4$-inch (6 mm) hardware cloth, and roll or fold into a tube approximately $11/2$ inches (3.8 cm) in diameter to form arms.

4

Wire the arms onto the column 8 inches (20.3 cm) from the top, across from each other, one on each side.

5

Cut a small piece of $1/4$-inch (6 mm) hardware cloth, approximately 8 inches (20.3 cm) square.

6

Fold under one end about 2 Inches (5.1 cm) to begin to define a chin. Bend the piece to form a curve for the face. Wire onto the base tube so that it protrudes slightly.

7

Cut another piece of $1/4$-inch (6 mm) hardware cloth approximately 12 x 30 inches (30.5 x 76.2 cm). Fold it in half lengthwise, and bend it to make a layer to form the hair. Wire it to the top of the tube starting at the sides of the face mesh so it hangs about 1 inch (2.5 cm) above the top of the arm sleeves.

8

For each change of plan (volume) you want to create in your figure, add a section of mesh and wire. When you finish the armature, it should resemble the structure or gesture you want the finished figure to have. Keep the armature fairly simple and smaller in volume than you want the finished form to be.

9

Continue to follow the instructions for Simple Column Armature, Chapter 2, pages 41 through 42, steps 9 through 14. Take particular care to fill the wire mesh additions that will begin to give your figure form. It's normal for the first application of concrete to look rough and for the figure to look awkward.

10

Turn the base form on its side, and determine where the electric cord for the pump will be located. Use the grinder with the masonry wheel to grind a channel on the underside of the foot and through the central core.

11

Insert a piece of flexible hose temporarily, to keep this channel open as you continue to concrete the form.

12

Mix the concrete and slurry for the second layer.

13

Spray the surface with water, and paint the slurry over the area where you plan to apply concrete.

14

Add concrete to begin to build up your form. Refer to Chapter 2: Direct Modeling, pages 55 through 57.

15

You can finish modeling the figure and apply the desired surface texture with the third application of concrete. Refer to Chapter 3: Surface Treatments for various options. This piece includes a combination of embedding and incising.

16

When finished, cover the figure with plastic and cure for one week. Remove the hose from the base.

Forming the Hat/Fountain Bowl

1

Follow instructions 1 through 5 and 7 for Sand Casting in Chapter 2, pages 37 through 39. The bowl for this piece should be deeper than a birdbath's to accommodate the fountain pump.

2

Make a bowl connection similar to the one described on page 39, but with following modification. Include the PVC pipe in the center of the basic bowl form. This pipe functions two ways: it works as an overflow if the water gets too high in the bowl, and it provides a space for the plug and cord to go through the center of the column rather than hang over the side of the bowl.

3

Use the table knife to carve a hole in the center of the sand to the table. Insert the piece of PVC pipe so that it rests on the table and protrudes 6 inches (15.2 cm) above the sand. This pipe remains in the bowl once it's cast.

4

Cut a hole in the middle of the dry-cleaning bag, and slide it over the pipe to cover the sand.

5

Cut a hole in the center of the reinforcing material, and set aside. Continue to follow steps 8 through 12, page 38.

6

To add the cup that will help attach the bowl to the figure in the final installation, first cut off the bottom of the cup. Slide it over the pipe, and center. Take small amounts of concrete and begin to fill the cup, taking care to tamp in the concrete as you go to eliminate any air pockets.

7

When you've finished, check the pipe and cup to make sure they're straight.

8

Pull up the edges of the dry-cleaning plastic around the bowl, and lay an unopened trash bag over the casting. Leave it undisturbed overnight.

9

Finish the sand casting process by completing steps 13 through 19, pages 38 through 39.

Forming the Crown of the Hat

1

The crown of the hat also functions to conceal the pump and the pipe. To form this, start with the small mixing

bowl to cast the shape. The inside of the bowl will be the size of the base form for the crown. It needs to be able to cover the pipe and the pump.

2

Spray the inside of the bowl with the aerosol lubricant.

3

Mix your concrete. Tamp about 1 inch (2.5 cm) of the concrete into the bottom of the bowl. Continue to form additional concrete up the sides to a thickness of about ³/₄ inch (1.9 cm).

4

Cut the alkali-resistant mesh into 3-inch (7.6 cm) pieces, and press into the concrete as if you were doing papier-mâché, overlapping the pieces. If you rub the mesh into the concrete with a circular motion, the pieces will embed more easily. They don't need to be completely covered but should look like they have a thin coating of concrete on them when you're finished. Cover the bowl with plastic, and leave undisturbed overnight.

5

The next morning, uncover the bowl, turn it upside down on the worktable, and tap it lightly as if you're

trying to get a loaf of bread out of its baking pan; it should drop right out.

6

Locate the center of the cast bowl form, and use the ¹/₂-inch (1.3 cm) masonry bit on your drill to slowly and carefully drill through the casting. This is where you'll position the brass fitting when you assemble the fountain.

7

Insert a small piece of flexible hose into the hole temporarily to keep it open when adding concrete. Remove when the piece is finished.

8

Consider the surface treatment options. Prepare any materials to use for embedding. When finished, cover the piece with plastic and allow to cure for one week.

Assembling the Fountain

1

Position the figure. Take the bowl and insert the cast cup stem with the pipe into the corresponding cast cup hole at the top of the figure.

2

Set the pump next to the pipe in the bowl, and thread the cord down the pipe and through the center of the figure. With someone helping, tip the figure slightly so you can pull the cord out of the center of the figure and align it with the precut channel.

3

Measure the height of where the pump sits in the bowl to the top of the hat crown, and cut a piece of flexible tubing that will fit securely onto the pump's water outlet and the base of your brass fitting.

4

Attach the tubing to the fitting, and slide it into the hole at the top of the crown. Tip the crown so there's room to maneuver, and attach the tubing to the pump. Reposition the crown.

5

Fill the bowl with water, and plug in the pump. Adjust the pressure of the pump as needed.

Totem for Alice

Literature is full of rich stories and references that can provide inspiration when you design a piece of artwork. Lewis Carroll's book *Through the Looking Glass* provided the symbols used to make this stacked sculpture: the Cheshire cat, the heart for the Queen, and of course, the white pawn for Alice.

MATERIALS & TOOLS

CONCRETE MIX: Premixed Sand (Topping) Mix or Mortar Mix or Mix 3
— Reverse-Cast Mosaic materials and tools (see page 73)
— Polystyrene Foam Waste Mold materials and tools (see page 35)
— Block of wood
— Sponge
— 1-inch (2.5 cm) galvanized pipe, 18 inches (45.7 cm) long
— Tape measure
— Metal-cutting saw
— ³/₄-inch (1.9 cm) stainless-steel rod

INSTRUCTIONS

Mosaic designs are reverse cast for one side of each piece, while the image on the opposite side is applied with a modified embedding process. When you work on this type of piece, it's a good idea to have all the mosaic designs and the molds completed before working with the concrete. You might want to cast two or three sections at a time to be efficient; however, if you try to cast more than that in one work session, you might find the process a little overwhelming.

1
Draw the shapes of the totem elements. Keep in mind that thin or extended areas may be hard to cast or balance, so try to keep each element blocky and similar in mass.

2
Cut out your paper templates, and lay them on the floor, or tack them to the wall so you can better visualize your totem.

3
Create a waste mold for each element, following steps 1 through 5 in the instructions for Adapting a Polystyrene Foam Waste Mold for a Totem Construction, page 36.

4

Follow the instructions in Chapter 3: Reverse-Cast Mosaic, pages 73 through 75, steps 1 through 13, for each piece. Create a different mosaic design for each side of each piece, or make the same design for each side.

5

Return to the instructions for Adapting a Polystyrene Foam Waste Mold, pages 36 through 37, and continue with steps 8 and 9, except only fill the mold to within ¼ inch (6 mm) of the top.

6

Position the second design for each element onto the surface of the castings, glaze side up. Use the block of wood to tap the design even with the top edge of the mold.

7

Allow to set until all the water has evaporated from the surface.

8

Remove the adhesive shelf paper. Rub small handfuls of concrete between the spaces of the embedded designs to fill the spaces (as if you were grouting). Take care not to push the design pieces in too deeply. If pieces appear to be sinking, stop and let the concrete continue to set.

9

Wipe the surface smooth and clean with a slightly damp sponge, and allow the castings to set up for 8 to 12 hours.

10

Follow steps 14 through 20 of Reverse-Cast Mosaic, pages 74 through 75.

11

Spray the castings, cure for five days, and allow to air dry.

12

To install the totem, set the 18-inch (45.7 cm) galvanized pipe into the ground in a concrete footing so that the pipe is true and vertical, and the top edge of the pipe is level with the footing.

13

Take the total measurement of your elements and the length of the pipe in the footing, subtract 2 inches (5.1 cm), and cut your stainless-steel rod to this length.

14

Position the first element over the hole of the footing and slide in the rod. With the aid of an assistant and the use of a sturdy ladder, slide each element over the rod.

Venetian Bench

You don't really have to go to Venice to enjoy this garden bench. Just imagine you're there as you sit on the colorful marble surface. A local marble installer let me rummage through his scrap pile to select a variety of colors and shapes to cast into a home-made mold—an installer's trash turned into treasure. Now all that's needed are the gondolas and canals.

MATERIALS & TOOLS

CONCRETE MIX: Premixed Sand (Topping) Mix, Mortar Mix, or Mix 3; Mix 1

- Tape measure
- Saw
- Plywood
- 26 linear feet (8 m) 2 x 4 stock
- 21 linear feet (6.5 m) 3/4-inch (1.9 cm) quarter-round molding
- Metal-cutting saw
- 18 linear feet (5.5 m) 1/2-inch (1.3 cm) rebar
- Sandpaper
- File
- Rusty metal primer
- Scissors or tin snips
- Roof flashing
- Screwdriver
- Drywall screws
- Hammer
- 3/4-inch (1.9 cm) wire brads with heads
- Common nails
- Try square
- 1 1/4-inch (3.2 cm) finishing nails
- Nail set
- Water-soluble white glue
- Mold release agent
- Roofing paper (tar paper)
- Wooden shim
- Assorted marble scraps
- Water-soluble white glue
- Small and large containers to mix concrete
- Screed
- Float
- Trowel
- 4 metal rods, 1/2 inch (1.3 cm) in diameter

CUT LIST FOR MOLD MATERIALS

Bench Leg Molds

Double the quantities if you wish to cast both legs at the same time.

Code	Description	Qty	Material	Size
A	Work Board	1	3/4" (1.9 cm) plywood	24 x 24" (61 x 61 cm)
B	Sides	2	2 x 4 stock	14" (35.6 cm)
C	Top & Bottom	2	2 x 4 stock	24" (61 cm)
D	Bracket Pieces	4	2 x 4 stock	3" (7.6 cm)
E	Curve Support	2	2 x 4 stock	see figure 1
F	Curve Support	2	2 x 4 stock	see figure 1
G	Curve Support	2	2 x 4 stock	see figure 1
H	Metal Curve	2	roof flashing	3 1/2 x 11 3/8" (8.9 x 28.9 cm)
I	Braces	4	2 x 4 stock	3" (7.6 cm)
J	Reinforcing	3	rebar	13" (33 cm)

Top of Bench Mold

Code	Description	Qty	Material	Size
K	Work Board	1	3/4" (1.9 cm) plywood	24 x 48" (61 x 122 cm)
L	Sides	2	2 x 4 stock	1 1/2 x 2 3/4 x 45" (3.8 x 7 x 114.3 cm)
M	Ends	2	2 x 4 stock	1 1/2 x 2-3/4 x 27" (3.8 x 7 x 68.6 cm)
N	Bracket Pieces	4	2 x 4 stock	3" (7.6 cm) long
O	Side Edge	4	1/4" (6 mm) molding	3/4 x 3/4 x 45" (1.9 x 1.9 x 114.3 cm)
P	End Edge	4	1/4" (6 mm) molding	3/4 x 3/4 x 15" (1.9 x 1.9 x 38.1 cm)
Q	Braces	2	2 x 4 stock	2 1/2" (6.4 cm)
R	Braces	4	2 x 4 stock	3" (7.6 cm)
S	Reinforcing	3	rebar	40" (101.6 cm)
T	Template	1	plywood	3 1/2 x 12" (8.9 x 30.5 cm)

INSTRUCTIONS

Constructing the Base Mold (see figure 1 on page 132)

1

Cut the mold materials as specified in the cut list. Sand or file the cut edges to remove splinters or loose materials, and spray the rebar with the primer.

2

Place two bracket pieces (D) flush at the ends of both the top and bottom boards (C). Attach each bracket with two screws.

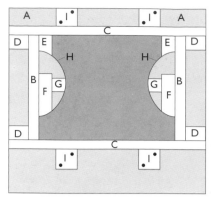

Figure 1

3

Attach the metal curve strip (H) to curve support (E) using two wire brads. Attach curve support (E) to the sides (B).

4

Attach curve supports (F) and (G) together as seen in figure 1, and secure to the sides boards (B) by screwing through section (F) with two screws. Attach the metal curve strip to section (F) with two wire brads so that the metal is flush against the side support.

5

Position the work board (A). Attach two brace pieces (I), 5 inches (12.7 cm) from each side, along the long edge of the work board.

6

Measure 17 inches (43.2 cm) from the top, and attach two more brace pieces (I) 5 inches (12.7 cm) from each side.

7

Cut a piece of roofing paper with the scissors to 16 x 17 inches (40.6 x 43.2 cm).

8

To assemble the mold, start with your work board positioned as described above. Center the roofing paper with the 17-inch (43.2 cm) side next to the braces. Position the sides, with curve support (E) at the top, inside the bracket supports of the top and bottom, and square up the pieces.

Constructing the Top Mold (see figure 2)

1

Cut your materials as specified in the cut list. Sand or file the cut edges to remove splinters or loose materials, and spray rebar with rusty metal primer.

2

Place bracket pieces (N) flush at the ends of the end boards (M). Attach each bracket with two screws.

3

Attach the side edge quarter-round molding pieces (O) to the side boards (L) so that the ends are flush and a flat side of the quarter-round molding lines up with the top edge and sides of side board (L). Secure the quarter-round with the finishing nails.

4

Measure and mark, using the try square, 4½ inches (11.4 cm) from each side of the end boards (M). Attach the end section of quarter-round (P) so that the corners of the quarter-round are lined up on the marked line, and a flat side of the quarter-round is lined up with the top edge and side of the end boards (M). Secure the quarter-round with finishing nails.

5

Position the work board (K) so that the 24-inch (61 cm) lengths are on the sides. Attach one support brace (Q), center with the 3½-inch (8.9 cm) side flush with the edge. Attach two braces (R) to both the top and bottom, 14 inches (35.6 cm) from each side, and flush to the edges.

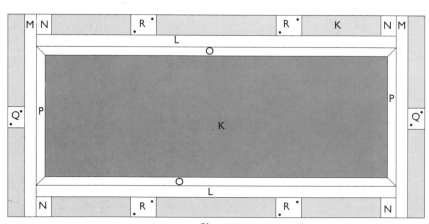

Figure 2

6

Cut a piece of roofing paper 18 x 43 inches (45.7 x 109.2 cm).

7

To assemble the mold, lay down the work board. Center the roofing paper onto the board. Position the end boards inside the side brace and slide the side boards into place. Slide the wood shims between the side braces and the board to tighten the mold.

Casting the Bench

1

Prepare the marble design. Draw out a rectangle the size of your bench. Taking into account the quarter-round edge, draw a line as a border guide 1-inch (2.5 cm) all the way around. Arrange your marble pieces. Marble or stone scraps may present more of a challenge for manipulating or shaping, however, if you have access to a masonry saw, you can get quite intricate with your design. A cold chisel and hammer are very helpful in breaking larger pieces into workable irregular shapes. Regardless of which method you use, be sure to wear safety goggles as you prepare your materials.

2

Once you have your pieces, tack them upside down with a small amount of the white glue onto the tar paper, and allow to dry.

3

Brush the mold release agent onto all interior surfaces of the wooden mold. The roofing paper will release easily from the casting without additional mold release.

4

Mix concrete mix 3. Apply the concrete in and around the marble pieces in the same manner as described in Reverse Casting, page 74, step 11. Also, apply a thin layer of concrete to the bench leg mold so that the texture and color of the bench parts match.

5

Mix concrete mix 1. Fill the molds half way and then

lay in the cut rebar (J, S) to reinforce the sections. Continue to fill the molds, taking care that the corners have been filled. Gently tap the edges of the mold to remove air bubbles. Level the top with the screed and then trowel smooth.

6

Allow all the surface water to evaporate and for the concrete to set before covering with plastic. Leave undisturbed for two to three days.

7

Unscrew and remove all the bracket pieces. Remove the sides and ends of the molds carefully by pulling the pieces straight away from the mold. Tap gently with the hammer if pieces appear to be stuck. Cure the bench sections for one week before assembling.

Assembling the Bench

1

Make the wooden template (T). This is the size of the top surface of the bench support. Drill 1/2-inch (1.3 cm) holes 2 inches (5.1 cm) in from each side and along the center line.

2

Positions the template on the top of the bench support, and mark the locations of the holes. With the masonry drill bit, drill 3-inch-deep (7.6 cm) holes that are true and perpendicular.

3

On the underside of the bench, measure 9 inches (22.9 cm) from each side and draw a line. Line up the hole on the line and center the template to mark your holes. Drill with the masonry bit 1 1/2-inch-deep (3.8 cm) holes that are true and perpendicular.

4

Insert the metal pins into the support holes. Position the supports onto a level location.

5

With the help of an assistant or two, line the bench holes over the support pins and set in place. Square the legs to steady the bench.

Figurative Table Base

Designer: Elder G. Jones

You've honed your carving skills making stepping stones and planters; now here's a chance to make a powerful statement. This abstract figure is carefully balancing the glass top on its head and legs, creating a table that looks equally elegant in the home or garden.

MATERIALS & TOOLS

CONCRETE MIX: Premixed Sand (Topping) Mix or Mix 4

— Tape measure

— Handsaw

— ³/₄-inch (1.9 cm) plywood

— 2 x 4 stock

— 4 pipe clamps

— 8 "C" clamps

— Plastic work board

— Mold release agent

— Large container to mix concrete

— Large knife or machete

— Assorted carving tools

— Nylon moving straps

INSTRUCTIONS

When designer Elder Jones created this piece, he had the clay model already designed. He calculated the scale of the piece and the size to build his form from the model. After the concrete was cast and the form was removed, he carved rather intensely for four hours. At that point, he had finished the sculpture, and the material was beginning to get too hard to work with.

1

Decide on the size of the base, and measure and cut the plywood for the sides and ends of the mold.

2

Butt the boards together to form a rectangle. Brace the form with the 2 x 4s and the clamps.

3

Place the form and the work board onto a sturdy table. Arrange your work area so that you'll be casting and carving at a comfortable height. A sturdy, low worktable with locking casters will make it easier to work and convenient to move outside when you're fin-ished. A moving pallet leveled on four milk crates, covered with a piece of ³/₄-inch (1.9 cm) plywood works also.

4

Apply the mold release to the inside of the form.

5

If you're using the premixed sand mix, first sift the dry ingredients through a window screen to remove large particles. Mix the concrete.

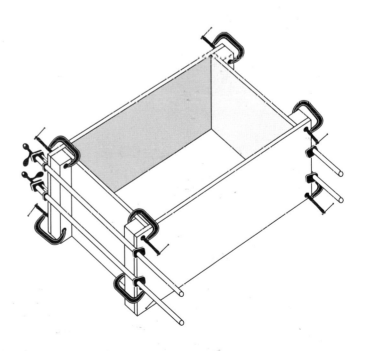

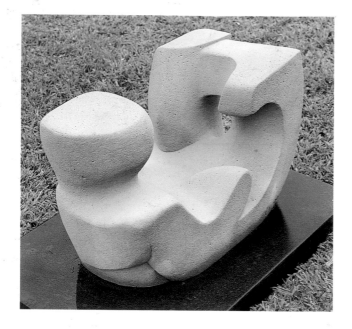
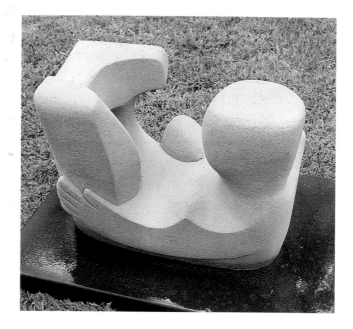

6

Fill the form. Tamp the form as you fill it in to eliminate air pockets.

7

Let the casting set three to four hours, or until it is firm enough to remove the form and retain its shape. Undo the pipe clamps and remove the plywood.

8

Use the large knife or machete to rough out the shape of the base by pressing the sharp edge through the cast block to shave off layers. Work the piece in the round, moving systematically around the piece to develop it evenly at each stage.

9

Remove all of the surface residue with a saw blade.

10

Refer to Chapter 2: Carving Basics, pages 50 through 51 and follow the instructions for Wet Carving on pages 52 through 54.

11

Leave the carved base uncovered and undisturbed overnight.

12

The next day, take the piece outside and hose it down to remove any debris from the surface. Bear in mind that the concrete is still fragile; use nylon moving straps and get a friend to help you move the base.

13

Cure the base for one week by hosing it with water several times a day or by wrapping it in wet cloths and covering with plastic.

Bird Watching

What are some of your favorite birds to watch? Combine them in a totem as you exercise your skills in building columns and polystyrene foam armatures. The idea is to create concrete pieces that fit together in a specific way, almost interlocking, to give the appearance of one piece rather than a group of smaller pieces that have been stacked.

MATERIALS & TOOLS

CONCRETE MIX: Premixed Sand (Topping) Mix, Mortar Mix, or Mix 3; Mix 10; Slurry Mixes 14 and 16

You'll need the tools and materials listed for the following techniques:

— Simple Column Armature, page 41

— Carving a Polystyrene Foam Armature, page 47

— Adapting a Polystyrene Foam Core for a Totem Construction, page 49

— Polymer-Fortified Concrete System, page 58

— Mosaic, page 68

— PVC pipe

— Grinder with masonry wheel

— 2 mil plastic

— Metal-cutting saw

— 1-inch (2.5 cm) diameter heavy galvanized pipe

INSTRUCTIONS

Base Trunk Construction

1

Construct the base following instructions 1 through 15 for Simple Column Armature, pages 41 through 42.

2

Mix the concrete and apply it to the armature. Cover and leave overnight.

3

The next day, use the file and the rubbing block to smooth off rough or thin areas and to refine the shape.

4

If you want to add more volume to the form or give added definition to the shape, add more concrete. Spray the piece with water, mix the slurry and concrete, and repeat steps 2 and 3. This is just a very basic construction. See Fitting the Pieces on page 139 to finish the form.

Constructing the Birds and Top Piece

1

Cut and carve the birds from polystyrene foam, Chapter 2: Carving a Polystyrene Foam Armature, pages 47 through 49.

2

Follow the instructions for Adapting a Polystyrene Foam Core for a Totem Construction, pages 49 through 50.

3

Carve the top piece in the same manner as the birds, but refer to the Bluebird/Pink House project: Pink House, steps 2 through 4 to insert the PVC pipe (page 120).

4

Cover the birds and the top piece with the polymer-fortified concrete system, pages 58 through 60, using small strips and squares of the lightweight mesh.

5

Cover with plastic and leave undisturbed overnight.

6

The next day use the rasp to remove rough spots and refine the shape.

7

Mix slurry 16 and concrete mix 10. Apply the concrete to the bird forms as needed to refine the shape.

Constructing Additional Sections

1

Cut pieces of PVC pipe a little longer than you want the finished sections.

2

Wrap the pieces of pipe generously with 20-gauge wire to within 1 inch (2.5 cm) on each end.

3

Mix slurry mix 14 and concrete mix 3. Brush on the slurry, and then apply the concrete by pressing it into the wrapped wire as you and begin to build up the form. Cover with plastic until the next day.

4

If you'd like to add more volume to the piece, wrap with wire in the same manner described above. If you'll just be adding a small amount of concrete, you don't need to wrap the wire.

5

Mix the same slurry and concrete, and apply to the sections.Cover with plastic until the next day.

Fitting the Pieces

1

You'll need to work with the concrete pieces so they'll fit together the way you want them to in the finished piece before you begin to mosaic. Start with the base and your first bird. Set the bird onto the base to see how it rests. You have the choice of either removing concrete to help it fit better, adding concrete, or using a combination of both.

2

To remove the concrete, use the grinder with the masonry wheel. Determine the direction you want the bird to be positioned. Draw on the surface of the base where the breast and tail of the bird curve down by drawing a line that is parallel to those contours. Remove the bird and begin grinding. Continue to try to fit the bird by checking the position as you work and grind, as needed.

3

At some point, you might want to add material to help the fit. Mix slurry 14 and concrete 3. Cover the bird in a piece of thin plastic so you don't end up cementing the two pieces together. Dampen and then slurry the base in the area you're trying to fit. Using small amounts of concrete, pack it into the area between the base and the plastic-covered bird. Leaving the bird in place, cover the base with plastic and leave undisturbed overnight.

4

The next day, carefully remove the bird. Use the file or rasp to refine the shape, adding more concrete to reinforce the form if necessary. Be careful not to add concrete onto the contoured edge created by the bird.

5

The next section will be fitting a spacing section onto the back of the bird. Again employ the carving and adding processes until you're satisfied. Consider how each piece will relate to one another as you fit them. When you've finished, you won't be able to adjust the positions by simply moving a piece around.

6

Follow the above steps for each section, working on one junction at a time. When you've finished the top section, stack all the pieces again to make any minor adjustments.

Mosaic Surfaces

1

Prepare your materials in advance. This allows you to create a working rhythm with the mosaic process. The thin strips have been cut on a diamond water ceramic saw. The small pieces have been broken with a hammer and then cut or nipped with tile tools. The leaves have been carefully shaped using the tile nippers.

2

Follow Mosaic instructions in Chapter 3, pages 68 through 71. Note: The tighter the curves of the piece you want to cover with mosaic, the smaller the pieces of mosaic material need to be.

Assembling the Piece

1

Refer to the instructions for the Bluebird/Pink House Totem, page 119.

Garden Throne

A Place to Daydream

There's a special satisfaction when you attempt and complete a large-scale piece. It allows you to push what you thought were your limits and can propel you to further your creative adventures. Let your imagination run wild as you complete this sturdy, yet surprisingly lightweight throne, so that when it's finished, you'll have a special place to sit as you further your dreams.

MATERIALS & TOOLS

CONCRETE MIX: Concrete Mix 16; Slurry Mix 16

— Caulk gun

— Construction caulk adhesive

— Large common nails

You will need the tools and materials listed for the following techniques:

— Carving a Polystyrene Foam Armature, page 47

— Adapting a Polystyrene Foam Armature for a Totem, page 49

— Polymer-Fortified Concrete Systems, page 58

Additional (optional materials):

— Roll of paper to make a pattern

— 1-inch-diameter (2.5 cm) PVC pipe

— 2 polystyrene foam balls, 4 inches (10.2 cm) diameter

— 2 found lamp parts

— 2 glass balls with holes through the center

— 2 metal rods

INSTRUCTIONS

Blocks and scraps of polystyrene foam were glued together to build a starting form. The carving began intuitively and progressed symmetrically. The best way to tell if a chair or throne will be comfortable when it's finished, is to sit in it often while working on the form. And, if your chair is going outside, factor in at least this one consideration—drainage.

1

Design your throne. Start with either a large block of polystyrene foam, or use the caulk adhesive to glue sections together to form a chunky mass to begin carving. If you glue pieces together, use the contact method described on page 50, and pin the section with large common nails to help hold the pieces in place. It's best to allow the adhesive to set overnight before carving.

2

Follow the instruction in Chapter 2: Carving a Polystyrene Armature, pages 47 through 49.

3

Any additions to your throne, such as pipes, reinforcing metal, or fastening systems, should be inserted or attached to the polystyrene foam form before you begin to apply the concrete. This way, they're incorporated into the structure and will function more effectively. This throne had two PVC pipes inserted into the back to accommodate the decorative elements. In a sense, they function as mini-totems. The pipes were inserted into the back of the throne the full length of the chair so that water would drain through them, rather than collect in the chair.

4

Refer to Adapting a Foam Core for a Totem Construction, page 49, to form the decorative elements. Stylized birds and small spheres were used for this throne.

5

Once the throne is carved, follow the instructions for the Polyadam Concrete System, pages 58 through 60.

6

Even though the structure is large, you still want to apply the scrim and concrete to the whole surface. Start the scrim and concrete application on the bottom, and work your way up using the light/medium scrim, then the heavy-duty scrim.

7

The birds and small spheres were constructed using only the light/medium scrim since they're decorative rather than structural elements. A second coat of concrete was added to refine the form.

Assembling the Throne

1

Refer to the assembly instructions for Bluebird/Pink House, page 117.

Modified Mobius

Designer: Lynn Olson

It's hard to believe this elegant sculpture, with the soft colors and the satin-smooth surface, is actually made of concrete. Designer Lynn Olson has refined this polishing technique through years of exploration, and he shares it with you here. The technique of polishing concrete can be used to finish the surfaces of animal and figurative sculptures as well.

MATERIALS & TOOLS

CONCRETE MIX: Mixes 11 and 12; Slurry Mix 15

— Needle-nose pliers
— Angle wire cutters
— 18- or 20-gauge stainless-steel wire
— Plastic-covered work board
— 2 mil plastic
— Polishing a Sculpture materials and tools (page 64)

INSTRUCTIONS

1

Design your sculpture, and with the needle-nose pliers, create an armature out of the wire that resembles the form you have envisioned. Place the armature on the center of the work board.

2

Mix a batch of mix 11 until it is the consistency of modeling clay. Press the first application of fiber cement into the armature. You don't have to fill in all the spaces between the wires. Wrap the armature in plastic, and let it set overnight.

3

The next day, thread additional wire through the spaces of the armature, to provide another layer to the base form.

4

Mix the slurry and brush it onto the form.

5

Mix another small batch of mix 11. Add a second application to the form, filling in all voids and holes. This will bring the design closer to its final form. The third coat (or finish application) of mix 12 can be applied as soon as the second coat has set.

6

Follow steps 2 through 10 of the instructions for Polishing a Sculpture on pages 64 through 65.

Featured Artists

Designers

George E. Adamy is the inventor of the Polydam Concrete System and is the worldwide distributor of its products. He has taught the PCS to teachers and artists across the country.

Elder G. Jones fashions one-of-a-kind objects from concrete. Contact: P.O. Box 81, Readyville, Tennessee 37149; (615) 409-6005.

Lynn Olson develops techniques for using portland cement with fibers and steel as a direct modeling sculptural medium. He's the author of *Sculpting with Cement*. Contact: 4607 Claussen Lane, Valparaiso, Indiana 46383; (219) 464-1792.

Gallery Artists

Kem Alexander builds bowls, stepping stones, tiles, and concrete floors. Contact: 31.5 Patten Parkway, Chattanooga, TN 37402; (423) 267-2695; kemalexander@aol.com.

Virginia Bullman has parlayed a fascination with fragments into a career creating mosaic wall panels, reliefs, and sculpture. Contact: Virginia's Art, Etcetera, 2435 Tall Pines Lane, Hillsborough, North Carolina, 27278; (919) 933-4950.

Sue Chenoweth received her MFA in painting from Arizona State University and is interested in the collaborative process in public art. Contact: (602) 242-2693.

Dan Corbin's work can be viewed at www.corbinsculpture.com.

LaNelle Davis is a musician, artist, and full-time social worker. Contact: Virginia's Art, Etcetera, 2435 Tall Pines Lane, Hillsborough, North Carolina, 27278; (919) 933-4950.

Thomas Arie Donch is a sculptor specializing in community-built projects. Contact: www.interplaydesign.com.

Andrew Goss creates jewelry, sculpture, and websites. Contact: 781 Second Avenue West, Owen Sound, Ontario, N4K 4M2, Canada; (519) 371-1857; www.makersgallery.com/concrete.

Johan Hagaman has been sculpting in paper and concrete for more than ten years. Contact: 6123 Stonehaven Dr., Nashville, Tennessee 37215; (615) 661-8854; johagaman@aol.com. To view more of her work, go to www.zeitgeist-art.com.

Jack Hastings apprenticed with architect/muralist Conrad Albrizio and studied under Diego Rivera early in his career creating architecture-based art. Contact: (931) 598-0660; janda@cafes.net.

Craig Nutt's art is frequently featured in exhibits throughout the U.S. He also lectures on and teaches woodworking. Contact: www.mindspring.com/cnutt.

Roy Kanwit is a self-taught sculptor who has been carving stone for more than 30 years. See more of Kanwit's work at his Taconic Sculpture Park and Gallery in Spencertown, New York, or his website, www.taconic.net/kanwit.

Buddy Rhodes' San Francisco-based company manufactures handmade, hand-colored concrete products for indoor and outdoor use. Contact: (877) 706-5303; www.buddyrhodes.com.

Lilli Ann Killen Rosenberg's murals and sculptures can be seen throughout the U.S. Contact: 4001 Little Applegate Road, Jacksonville, Oregon 97530; (541) 899-7861.

Marvin Rosenberg has collaborated on dozens of commissioned works with his wife, Lilli Ann Killen Rosenberg.

Pedro Silva, a native of Chile with a studio in New York, New York, has completed several public art projects in ceramic tile mosaic. Contact: 165 Clermont Ave., Brooklyn, NY 11205; (718) 852-6143.

Nina Solomon's primary medium is clay, though cement and tile have become more important in public art. Contact: 1817 W. Northview Ave., Phoenix, Arizona 85021; (602) 995-0804; ninasolomon@yahoo.com.

Resources

Many of these resources deal primarily with industries but will work with individuals as best they can. Be as specific about the intended use as possible when ordering, or, if unsure, ask for a sample for experimentation. Most suppliers can provide catalogues or information sheets upon request.

Polyadam Concrete System Supplies, Alkali-Resistant Fiberglass Mesh (Glass Scrim)
George E. Adamy
11-1 Woods Brooke Circle
Ossining, New York 10562
(914) 941-1157

Alkali-Resistant Fiberglass Mesh, Polymers
Ball Consulting
338 14th Street
Ambridge, PA 15003
(800) 225-2673
or
1155 W. 23rd Street
Tempe, AZ 85282
(888) 967-7727
www.ball-consulting-ltd.com

Silica Fume and Air-Entraining Agents
Fox Industries, Inc.
3100 Falls Cliff Road
Baltimore, MD 21211
(888) 760-0369
www.fox-ind.com

1-Gallon (3.8 L) Containers of Air-Entraining Agent (called Trysta)
W.R. Grace & Co.
62 Whittemore Avenue
Cambridge, MA 02140
(617) 876-1400

Powdered Pigments
Daniel Smith
4150 First Avenue South
Seattle, WA 98124
(800) 662-2927

Other Pigments
Solomon Colors
4050 Color Plant Road
Springfield, IL 62702
(800) 846-2599
www.solomoncolors.com

Iron Oxide Colors
Arizona Oxides L.L.C.
12519 W. Butler Drive
El Mirage, AZ 85335
(800) 576-1500
www.arizonaoxides.com

Acid Stains
Kemiko
(903) 587-3708
www.kemiko.com

Increte Systems
(800) 752-4626
www.increte.com

Metakaolin
Engelhard Corporation
Pigments & Additives Group
101 Wood Avenue
Iselin, NJ 08830-0770

Polypropylene Fibers
SI Concrete Systems
4019 Industry Drive
Chattanooga, TN 37416
(800) 621-0444
www.fibermesh.com

Polystyrene Foam Cutting Tools
Demand Products, Inc.
1055 Nine North Drive
Alpharetta, GA 30004
(800) 325-7540
www.demandproducts.com

Bibliography

Andrews, Oliver. *Living Materials: A Sculptor's Handbook*. Berkeley, CA: University of California Press, 1988.

Beardsley, John. *Gardens of Revelation: Environments by Visionary Artists*. New York: Abbeville Press Inc., 1995.

Niles, Susan A. *Dickeyville Grotto: The Vision of Father Mathias Wernerus*. Jackson, MS: University Press of Mississippi, 1997.

Quikrete Companies Staff. *Build and Repair with Concrete: The Complete Do-It-Yourself Manual*. Atlanta, GA: The Quikrete Companies, 1992.

Professional Organizations

These organization can provide technical information and help find additional resources.

American Concrete Institute
38800 Country Club Drive
P.O. Box 9094
Farmington Hills, MI 48333
(248) 848-3800

Portland Cement Association
5420 Old Orchard Road
P.O. Box 726
Skokie, IL 60076
(800) 868-6733

Related Websites
www.concretenetwork.com
www.concrete.com
www.makersgallery.com/concrete

To contact the author, Sherri Warner Hunter:

3375 Fairfield Pike
Bell Buckle, TN 37020
sherriartstudio@aol.com

Index